TEACHING YOUR FIRST COLLEGE CLASS

TEACHING YOUR FIRST COLLEGE CLASS

A Practical Guide for New Faculty and
Graduate Student Instructors

Carolyn Lieberg

STERLING, VIRGINIA

Sty/us

COPYRIGHT © 2008 BY
STYLUS PUBLISHING, LLC.

Published by Stylus Publishing, LLC
22883 Quicksilver Drive
Sterling, Virginia 20166–2102

Library of Congress Cataloging-in-Publication-Data
Lieberg, Carolyn S.
  Teaching your first college class : a practical guide for new faculty and graduate student instructors / Carolyn Lieberg.—1st ed.
    p.   cm.
Includes bibliographical references and index.
ISBN 978-1-57922-225-3 (cloth : alk. paper)—
ISBN 978–1-57922-226-0 (pbk. : alk. paper)
1. College teaching—Handbooks, manuals, etc.
2. College teachers. 3. First year teachers.
I. Title.
LB2331.L48   2008
378.1'25—dc22   2007025440

ISBN: 978-1-57922-225-3 (cloth)
ISBN: 978 1 57922 226-0 (paper)

Printed in the United States of America

All first editions printed on acid free paper
that meets the American National Standards Institute
Z39-48 Standard.

Bulk Purchases

Quantity discounts are available for use in workshops and for staff development.
Call 1-800-232-0223

First Edition, 2008

10 9 8 7 6 5 4 3 2 1

This book is dedicated to
Ernest Boyer, Cleo Martin, and Tom Rocklin

CONTENTS

ACKNOWLEDGMENTS

I never could have written this book without the instructors and developers who, over the years, have given a great deal of thought and attention to teaching and to learning. I am grateful to those known and unknown who engaged in casual conversations or undertook research projects, those who passed along their ideas informally and those who published articles and books to add to the catalog of ideas about effective instruction. My contact with members of POD—the Professional Organization of Faculty Development Network in Higher Education—was an extraordinarily helpful resource, whether through conferences, publications, phone calls, or Listservs.

For aid in the writing of this book, I want to thank those who facilitated my sleuthing. I also want to to express specific gratitude to several developers and professors who took time to encourage me and to respond to my questions. They include Donald Wulff, Larry Michaelsen, Nancy Hauserman, Anthony Brunello, Fred Antczak, Deborah Schoenfelder, Nancy Hinman, Denise Camin, David Perlmutter, and Jean Florman. Thanks, too, to John von Knorring, president and publisher of Stylus Publishing and Judy Coughlin, who shepherded me through the production phase.

My acknowledgments would be hollow without publicly paying tribute to Cleo Martin, my teaching mentor, whose faith and confidence in me, when I was a novice graduate instructor at the University of Iowa, made all the difference. She changed my life. I also benefited in many ways from my work under Ernest Boyer. His patience, wit, and wisdom made it a pleasure to work with him; his encouragement of the highest ideals made it an honor. Last, the director of the Center for Teaching at the University of Iowa, Tom Rocklin, created an atmosphere where discussions about teaching and learning flowed easily through our days, and inquiries into old ideas or suggestions for new ones were always entertained. I could not have asked for a more ideal mentor for faculty development. Tom, thank you.

I

BEGINNINGS

Welcome to the other side of the desk.

As a **Novice College Teacher**, you are about to embark on **The Bold Enterprise** that you have been watching others fulfill for years. As with the assumption of any new role, it is quite natural to have **Apprehensions and Trepidations,** but you are also excited about the opportunities before you, which include **The "It" Factor—Help Students Understand What It Means to Be Educated.** Most new faculty are hired in an assistant status where they look forward to the years of work that will lead to tenure. On the other hand, Graduate Student Instructors (GSIs) are hired in many **Types of Appointments** that determine both income and instructional responsibilities. Regardless of how much or how little teaching you do, this book is designed to offer support and ideas in many areas. You can also find **Help for Your Teaching** from a range of people and sources on your campus.

A s a new instructor—GSI or faculty member—you are about to adopt a complex and exciting role. This book is designed to be a guide for dealing with many of the issues instructors encounter in their first year of college teaching. Throughout, you'll find strategies and suggestions for handling practical issues. Some sections deal with philosophical and theoretical material that will enrich your knowledge of varied aspects of education and inform your daily teaching. We hope that you will be able to blend your past educational experiences and ideas with the content presented here to create a foundation for your new position.

On Being a Novice College Teacher

No other teaching experience will feel quite like the first time you walk into a classroom to face a fresh class of students. Similar to other new adventures, the moment is filled with excitement, hope, and perhaps some feelings of apprehension. The act of teaching will rarely be so freighted with emotions as it is during that first session.

Some new college instructors have the advantage of temperament or experience that allows them to enter a classroom in a state of calm and confidence. This minority includes people who have done a lot of public speaking and those who have taught in other venues. Many teachers are initially uneasy, but being nervous does not prevent novice teachers from engaging students or from initiating activities that will make your students feel part of a community of learners.

New instructors often express concerns about their students—will they be interested or bored, eager or apathetic, or will they be returning adult students who are older than their teachers? You may also wonder about syllabus preparation, grading requirements of the institution, and how you'll succeed in running your discussion section. Nearly everyone has anxieties about something. On the other hand, most instructors are excited about sharing the knowledge of their discipline and about the very idea of teaching.

With so many responsibilities pressing on new instructors, it is no surprise that new teachers feel anxious. An informal survey of some GSIs revealed that, in addition to the issues above, instructors wondered about establishing a rapport with students, getting them to attend class regularly and do the homework, and how they would deal with plagiarism.[1]

Each of these topics will be covered in this book, both in a practical way and by considering some of the theories that underlie educational activities. We hope that these threads of practice and theory will provide you with the resources to proceed confidently into this many splendored thing that is teaching.

The Bold Enterprise

Whether you are a graduate student in pursuit of a degree or you are a new faculty member, this move into teaching represents one more adventure in the activities of a scholar. You may be anticipating new areas of study and associations with illustrious professors or researchers. Perhaps you have relocated to a place you barely know.

---

[1] My thanks to Suzanne Swiderski who, as she was completing her EdD at the University of Iowa, asked peers at Iowa and around the country about the apprehensions they had when they were new GSIs.

The excitement of new ventures serves the good purpose of easing some of the tensions of transplanting oneself, and perhaps one's family, to a new job and even a new city. Inevitably such a change demands that you cope with large and small details, but the energy itself of the bold leap helps you deal with the unexpected. So it is with teaching.

Apprehensions and Trepidations

In any fresh undertaking, things will go wrong or at least take surprising turns: it's unavoidable. Maintaining an expectation that there *will* be obstacles will help enormously when they arise. Many of them will be connected to your teaching and may include such things as offices being closed at odd hours, ordered books not arriving on time, delays in materials being placed on reserve at the library, audiovisual equipment malfunctions, computers or printers failing, crucial Web sites going down, and so on. These problems are common and occur to nearly everyone at some point. Other sorts of problems, such as not being able to find a parking place or missing a bus, are also to be expected. And it may happen that you overlook an important stack of papers you meant to bring to class—graded papers, a quiz, a handout for the day. Sometimes things go wrong. Life is like that, but there is no sense, as they say, in borrowing trouble by anticipating problems.

A much more common event that causes stress is public speaking—one of the most universal anxieties. Surveys that ask the general public what it fears most reveal that public speaking ranks in first or second place, competing with death. Knowing that other people are nervous does not ease one's own nerves. The act of speaking to a group is fraught with hurdles, especially if you've done it infrequently or if it's been awhile since it was part of your regular responsibilities.

As with other risky adventures, repeated experience is the best way to become comfortable and confident. The haunting question is what to do on the way to becoming experienced. Theater people advise us to breathe deeply and to look at the audience—really look—by making eye contact with individuals. They also suggest that you embrace some degree of performance anxiety because it gives a boost of energy that can help you speak more loudly and move yourself around the room. It is useful to learn some techniques for managing sensations of anxiousness. Organist Robert Triplett

(1983) recommends vocal exercises and shaking out the hands and arms to help shed jitters. It may feel silly, but it helps.

Beyond managing yourself, one highly effective way to ease the pressure of public speaking is, literally, to share it: It's easier to be part of a choir than to sing a solo. First-year students are also apprehensive about college—What will be expected of them? Will they make mistakes and feel foolish? What will their teachers be like?—and share many of the same concerns that new instructors have. Your first class may be a student's first class, too. Transfer some of the speaking responsibilities to students on the first day to relieve your anxiety and to set the expectation from the beginning that everyone is supposed to participate.

The "It" Factor—Help Students Understand What It Means to Be Educated

Many parts of teaching are greatly satisfying—watching students become engaged and excited about course topics and material, helping them untangle their confusions, and seeing them get it, whatever "it" is in your field, all contribute to the rewards of teaching. And it is a thrill, plain and simple, to provide students with ways to discover and explore knowledge—some students will find an enthusiasm they may not have imagined they had.

A very likely difference between those at the front of the room, whether faculty or graduate students, and those seated in the desks is the attitude toward learning. You and your peers have undertaken the mastery of new material, you want to understand new theories and conceptual frameworks and continue building your disciplinary expertise. New faculty are fairly bursting with the results of their graduate studies and the results of their dissertations. New undergraduates, on the other hand, are worlds away from you. They've been tested to death in their K–12 years, so it is not surprising that many arrive at college with the constant question: "Will this be on the test?" The corollary to that question seems often to breed a "learn it and lose it" attitude. Education for many of them has come to resemble a series of meals where ingredients are gathered, assembled, cooked, and eaten, and leftovers are tossed out. Then it's on to the next meal—or test. One of your challenges is to guide students away from that attitude toward one where they see themselves as educated adults who take pleasure in their accumulating knowledge and broadening understandings. Your enthusiasm and setting an example can provide a powerful inspiration.

Consider giving your students an architectural metaphor for their education—a construction with a malleable building material that allows for revising the building an infinite number of times (one imagines a computer modeling system rather than tangible concrete). Don't assume students understand this method of education; they are accustomed to simply piling on the bricks/credits without doing much modification of the whole structure. A good example of the need to reconfigure knowledge might be the Civil War. Young students are taught that it was about slavery, and it was. But it was also about secession and economics and varied beliefs of how to build a strong country (for instance, a Southern argument insisted that all great civilizations had been built on slave labor) and other factional issues. Design some examples from your own field to help students realize what "knowing" is and why scholars continue to study in order to improve and expand that knowing. It is always an unfinished task.

Courses, too, can seem to be delivered as discrete packages, whether in English, physics, or sociology. Some professors may provide wisps of a big picture, but students are rarely offered ways to organize their learning in order to make more of it fit together. When an opportunity arises where you can help students connect disparate pieces of knowledge, do so. A liberal education is, among other things, about a wide and deep understanding of the world. Helping students find ways to organize their thinking is a worthy teaching goal.

Types of Appointments

Depending upon the institution, the department, the funding sources, and one's ability to communicate in English, GSIs may find their first assignment to be

- Grading papers
- Participating in drop-in consultation or tutoring pools for students
- Assisting a professor in record keeping, Web site maintenance, scheduling, and so on
- Running a laboratory or studio or assisting in running one

- Running a section that meets one to three times a week in support of lectures given by a professor
- Running a complete class with all the concomitant responsibilities
- Supervising clinics
- Managing field placements

Generally graduate students are given a one-tenth to a one-half appointment, though your campus may designate these portions in a different manner. The one-tenth appointment may apply to graders, Web managers, or other types of assistants for professors. Percentages for teaching assignments vary by the number of classes, how often you meet with students, how many credits per course, and perhaps the number of students you are responsible for.

Regardless of your teaching assignment, the fact is that fulfilling the responsibilities well will most likely lead to more assignments with more responsibilities, which may in turn lead to increased financial reward and more experiences to draw from when you search for a permanent position. Even if you are not yet responsible for a class or a discussion section, many of the ideas in this book will strengthen your knowledge and your confidence in whatever interactions you may have with students, and assist you in doing good work for your professor or department.

Two Bosses or More

As with other employment, being a GSI or faculty member may mean having several bosses.

GSIs may have a teaching supervisor, the professor whose sections the GSI runs, and perhaps faculty members who run seminars on teaching sponsored by the department. If you work for a professor, you'll find that he or she has the lion's share of responsibility for how you handle the sections. You may find, unsurprisingly, that supervising faculty may offer conflicting suggestions about teaching. Sometimes you may have to abide by actions you don't like. As your experience grows, the contact and the directives you receive will help shape you as a teacher—either by good example or by actions that you resolve not to use when you have more independence.

Both GSIs and new faculty are also under the direction of department chairs, deans, provosts, presidents, chancellors, a board of regents, or other administrators and administrative groups. Meanwhile you will be overseeing students. Naturally, the best situation is when those who supervise you and those whom you supervise are content and believe you are attending to your duties competently.

Appointments Outside the Classroom

If your initial appointment consists of behind-the-scenes grading, record maintenance, or attending to matters on the Web, you can still gain benefits by "thinking like an instructor" about the matters you tend to. As a grader, you will learn about test preparation and methods. Do the examinations and quizzes fit the material well? Are they fair and do they, in your view, assess the knowledge that students should take away from the course? If you work on someone's Web site, you—being a more recent undergraduate than the faculty member you work for—can assess the clarity and expectations of the professor's instructions, materials, and postings.

If you are grading essays or short answers, do you see how student thinking is reflected in the answer—for better or for worse? Sometimes graders have the task of meeting with disgruntled students to review a test's answers. No one relishes grade conflicts, but they do offer an opportunity to help a student shift the focus away from an emotional reaction against the teacher and move it toward the misunderstood material.

Finally, you will be able to listen to other GSIs discuss their classes—the triumphs and frustrations. I know a woman who learned to play guitar by watching her friends practice and play; by the time she grasped a guitar neck in the fingers of one hand and strummed the strings with the fingers of the other, she seemingly could feel the rhythms and chords in her bones. Close and analytical observation is one indisputable way to learn.

Finding Help for Your Teaching

No single resource, human or otherwise, can solve every teaching problem, but there are many places to find aid. Sometimes peers, GSIs, or other faculty members have a ready solution. Most institutions or disciplines have Listservs for GSIs and/or faculty where questions can be posed and responded to. You may have a friend, even in another department, who would be willing to sit in on a class or two. GSIs can ask teaching supervisors for help, and department chairs may be helpful to faculty and GSIs.

A growing number of colleges and universities provide a center or office where teachers can seek help through consultation or resources. Some offices have large staffs and many workshops and other activities for instructors. Others exist on a smaller budget and are staffed on a part-time basis. Nevertheless, those who work there are well informed about teaching strategies and can offer you a range of ideas. The centers also have helpful resources, including books, videos, journals, and perhaps filming equipment for those who would like to be taped while teaching. The staff's overall goal is to support instructors. You will be well received, and your questions and concerns will be readily addressed.

While there is a great deal of valuable information available, remember that teaching is in many ways highly personal. If you hear or see a suggestion that simply doesn't sound right for you, don't force yourself into adopting it. If you hear about an appealing idea and you try it but find that it flops, push it to the back burner. Wait to try it again until you are more experienced or have a fresh class of students. You'll hear about plenty of strategies that you'll be able to implement with great success.

Reference

Triplett, R. (1983). *Stagefright: Letting it work for you.* Chicago: Nelson-Hall.

2

TEACHING INTENTIONALLY

As we know from our lives as students, some teaching characteristics stand out as signs of excellent teaching. **Success—Three
Brief Tips** offers unsurprising yet reassuring suggestions. In the
heart of teaching, where teachers mediate content, rests **Pedagogy,** the study of the ways we teach. One of the largest shifts in
pedagogy during the past few decades is a move away from
Teacher-Centered to Student-Centered classrooms. Instead of
presenting information to students and hoping they retain it, the
move means that teaching focuses on engaging students in **Active Learning** in the classroom. Social learning, which John
Dewey endorsed, calls for people to be challenged at the edges
of their knowledge and in their viewpoints, which contributes to
Critical Thinking. Using the course content to create activities for
students is one of **The Many Roles of Teachers. Some Major
Figures in Pedagogy** describes some of the thinking of a few of
the most important people in the field. Finally, instructors can give
Special Attention to Undergraduates and how they can learn
most effectively. **Making Use of Technology** may alter your established pedagogical methods and enhance learning opportunities for students.

It is not uncommon to hear new instructors say, "I feel as if I've been
thrown into the deep end of the pool." The statement is apt. Despite
the many years that every teacher has spent as a student, moving to the
other side of the desk is a shift with enormous and unexpected demands.

The first, and historical, expectation of professors is that they be well
versed in their field of knowledge, but the truth is that effective teaching
also depends upon clarity in expressing ideas, genuine communication with
students, astute planning, performance abilities, appropriate assignments and

exams, and more. Despite the breadth of abilities that good, experienced teachers rely upon, it is not at all uncommon for new GSIs and faculty to have successful teaching experiences. Their instructional history may be short, but enthusiasm and determination, accompanied by reflection on teaching methods and a willingness to adjust instructional tone when needed, provide potent tools to conduct an effective course. In essence, decisions about the kind of teacher you want to be leads to a philosophy of teaching, which then dictates how the art of teaching is practiced.

Success—Three Brief Tips

Not surprisingly, students give high ratings to instructors for enthusiasm, knowledge, and caring about students. The opportunity to express these attributes begins with the first class.

Enthusiasm

The way you introduce the course, how it fits into the discipline, the manner in which you talk about textbooks and assignments all reflect your attitude about the course topics and a great deal about your philosophies on teaching and learning. I spoke with a senior once who said that her favorite teacher had been a GSI she had had her freshman year. On the first day, the instructor spent a lot of time talking about the books they would be reading. He liked some of them very much, but a few presented material in a way that he objected to; he would argue against the author's ideas. On he went. The student said his passion and his honesty held the class in thrall, and the tone that he set that day lasted all semester.

Knowledge

GSIs often fear not knowing everything and being caught in their ignorance by wise or inquiring students. This fear needs to be managed. The time has long since passed when any single person knew everything about a discipline. Some people may know everything about a small slice of a discipline, but I have never heard anyone claim to know everything in a discipline. Expect to be asked questions you cannot answer. In some cases, it makes sense to ask students to search for information, and other times you may want to pursue answers yourself. What you can say is, "That's an interesting question," which shows that you care about learning. You do, in fact, know a great deal more than your students.

Caring

All of us feel cared about when people look at us when we speak and truly listen to our ideas or questions. Students also feel cared about if you show that you are accessible to them outside class. Fair tests and grading and appropriate assignments matter, too. The basic message is that students want to be treated with respect.

Pedagogy

The technical term for the philosophy of teaching is *pedagogy*. If you have studied education in some way, you will be familiar with the word. Depending upon your field (humanities—yes; business—not so much), you may hear faculty members and supervisors use the word a great deal or very little, with "teaching methods" or "way of teaching" as a substitute.

The word "pedagogy" comes to us through the French but derives from the Greek *paidagogia* (office of a pedagogue; the slave who accompanied a child to school; boy + guide). "Pedagogic" is the adjective, and neither it nor pedagogy carry a bias. On the other hand, "pedagogue" and "pedant" come from the more recent Latin *paedagogare* (to instruct), and both of them characterize what we hope to avoid—the type of teacher who focuses excessively on minor details to show off his or her learning.

There is a great deal to know about pedagogy, but, regardless of discipline, all GSIs and faculty can benefit by learning about some of the dominant ideas. Those briefly described below are derived from the work of John Dewey (1916), Lev Vygotsky (1978), Benjamin Bloom (1956), Robert B. Barr and John Tagg (1995), and of Arthur W. Chickering and Zelda F. Gamson (1987).

Pedagogy is, simply, the study of ways of teaching; the word encompasses theory and practice. Everyone who teaches uses theories about teaching—consciously or not—as they execute their practices. People often talk about their preferred pedagogy, by which they generally mean "practice" with the assumption that others can discuss the theory behind it.

Discussions of whether an education should prepare students to be good citizens or prepare them for the workplace have played key roles in the minds of teachers for a very long time. Such fundamental choices affect nearly all aspects of how we educate students.

In this era, a great deal of college teaching is leaning away from the old custom of instruction driven by the instructor as a deliverer of knowledge and toward methods of instruction driven by student learning. With this shift gaining increasing momentum, it is an exciting time to become a college instructor. Running a discussion section or leading a class, regardless of discipline, gives you an opportunity to initiate lots of opportunities for students to be active and engaged.

Teacher-Centered or Student-Centered

The differences between student-centered and teacher-centered classrooms stand out in stark relief in this old joke that continues to make the rounds in education circles. It goes something like this:

> A young man tells friends that he's taught his dog how to whistle.
>
> The friends, duly impressed, gather to witness the phenomenon but hear only "arfs."
>
> "Well," says the young man, "I said I *taught* him how to whistle, I didn't say he *learned* it."

The traditional pedagogical style in college has been the lecture, which persists as the norm in many places and in many disciplines; it can serve the purpose of presenting a great deal of information to large audiences of students in a relatively short time. We have all attended excellent and highly engaging lectures, but the fact that the teacher is teaching does not ensure that the students are learning. The student-centered classroom calls for students to be much more engaged than the typical auditorium of students. Many sections in this book address the practical applications of a student-centered pedagogy—from running discussions to using assignments and tests that require active engagement among the students.

You may hear GSIs or faculty say they feel as if they are not doing their jobs if student learning is at the center of the course. These same instructors may express the view that it is their job to present material, and it is up to the students to "get it"; they are college students, after all, and if they cannot sort things out . . . On it goes. In your own experience, can you recall a great teacher who was indifferent to students? Teaching well is inexorably linked to solid learning.

Think of classroom practices on a continuum. At one end is the image of a professor presenting a lecture to students whose alertness may be flagging as the minutes pass. At the other end of the line is a classroom abuzz with students exploring ideas, asking questions, talking and agreeing and disagreeing, whether the teacher is actively involved or simply observing the learning he or she has set in motion.

Along the continuum are many possibilities that make use of faculty members' or GSIs' expertise and creativity, including classroom activities, graphics organizers (flow charts, relational maps, and so on), group tests, spontaneous debates, and even the occasional mini-lecture. Students may be apprehensive about becoming heavily engaged as active learners because they may have experienced group work that bored them or that seemed like busy work. You may have to initiate some unexpected activities to capture their imagination, but the venture is worth it. In designing your class, you can *think* student-centered from the first day without abrogating your responsibilities or throwing students into their own proverbial deep end of the pool.

Teachers in Their Many Roles

Conducting a student-centered class means that you are more facilitator than information deliverer. To do this, you need to create activities that trigger curiosity and interest and that inspire learning. However, students are paying steep tuition bills, and they look to you for expert leadership. As their guide through the content and through the cognitive processes scholars use to evaluate information and viewpoints, you are invaluable to your students. Focusing on what they learn does not nullify the role of the teacher; rather it simply means that instead of preparing for class with the thought, "How can I best present this material?" you'll be thinking, "How can students best learn this material?" Sometimes these questions have overlapping answers.

You will very likely create useful activities for pairs and small groups, and occasionally you will give mini-lectures. Teaching from a learner-centered standpoint means that you attend to how much and how well the students are learning as you also attend to the course work. Teaching in this fashion is a dance between the posts of content and student progress, but since student-centered teaching offers more frequent information about the advancement of student learning, you will have a great advantage in helping students stay on track with the course material.

New instructors are in an excellent position to embrace student-centered learning, because, at this point, they have spent the bulk of their time as students. If you are among this group, classroom experiences, from a student's standpoint, are fresher in your mind. Unlike seasoned faculty, you have, for the most part, not spent a decade or more preparing and delivering lectures.

Active Learning

Active learning is essentially what it sounds like—high engagement behaviors that propel and energize student learning. The pedagogy encompasses teaching strategies that invite students to engage with one another to probe ideas and texts, solve problems of every sort, and challenge thinking.

Active learning provides opportunities for a wide range of group dynamics where students interact with their peers and instructors as they grapple with material to stretch understandings and forge broader comprehensions. Classrooms where active learning pedagogy is employed are places where students expect to participate in small- or large-group activities and where they know they will leave the session with their minds buzzing from the provocations, questions, and interactions.

Proponents of active learning—and it has become a dominant model in many classrooms in all disciplines—endorse the notion that people learn more by doing than by being passive. Activity (discussing points; asking and answering questions; working with others; preparing any sort of summary, reaction, or presentation) requires students to study the material and interact with the comments and thus the thinking of their peers. It pushes their abilities to think critically.

The biggest single feature of active learning is that it shifts the classroom focus away from the conventional "sage on the stage" toward students actively engaged in figuring something out.

Discussion sections of any sort offer an ideal laboratory for active learning. There are many potential ways of learning material. Your discipline may be suited to some strategies over others; over the length of a term, you can explore several teaching methods.

I've heard tales of rebellion among students who expect classes to be run in a traditional manner then learn that their class will be run differently. This unfortunate reaction has helped me decide that it may well be better simply to conduct a few active learning events in the natural course of things and let the successes accumulate. Once students experience the engagement and the rewards of involved learning, you might find an opportunity to talk about it, perhaps during a midterm classroom assessment. As an example in their own lives, you might ask them about the differences they found in reading about driving or watching others drive and actually getting behind the wheel themselves.

You should know, too, that some people in academia regard active learning as a way to ease young students into the culture of college learning. But active learning is about offering students intellectual challenges to solve rather than explaining to them how someone else already solved them.

Critical Thinking

One of the most discussed topics in education is critical thinking. Schools want students to acquire it, and employers want to hire college graduates who have it. Teaching people to think is obviously not like teaching them to draw triangles, but there are general principles that can help you facilitate the practice of this crucial skill in the minds of your students.

The term has been defined in many ways, but the one below from the Foundation and Center for Critical Thinking is attractively inclusive:

> Critical thinking is the intellectually disciplined process of actively and skillfully conceptualizing, applying, analyzing, synthesizing, and/or evaluating information gathered from, or generated by, observation, experience, reflection, reasoning, or communication, as a guide to belief and action. In its exemplary form, it is based on universal intellectual values that transcend subject matter divisions: clarity, accuracy, precision, consistency, relevance, sound evidence, good reasons, depth, breadth, and fairness. (Scriven & Paul, n.d.)

A question that instructors often have relates to whether undergraduates are prepared to learn to think critically. When students arrive at college, they have very likely passed through a phase of cognitive development called *dualistism*. As it sounds, the word is about viewing the world as a fairly clear duality—right/wrong or good/bad. While this manner of thinking is linked somewhat to the early teen years, it can persist well beyond then if it is not challenged. You can see many adults on any given television show whose ideas reveal that they continue to see the world in fairly black-and-white terms.

The next phase, as defined by William Perry (cited in Rapaport, 2006), Marcia Baxter Magolda (1998), and others is about multiplicity and subjectivity. Students understand that multiple views exist on a given issue, but they tend to believe that one view is correct (and they frequently want to be told what it is). Students need to be assured that indeed there are multiple interpretations, but these interpretations compete for dominance, and that in many cases, there is not a single, shining, right answer.

As students gain an understanding of this principle, try to crack open the door to the next level of thinking, which has been labeled *relativism* and has to do with students' recognizing that there are multiple interpretations and that they must choose one and understand why. Beyond this phase, students (upper division and beyond) gain an understanding in how to select a position and support and embrace it.

How can you best guide students toward this goal? Raise issues that are open-ended and do what you can to delay the students' leap to a right answer. Many topics in college lend themselves to pushing students along the path to critical thinking. The question "Why?" is the key. Robert J. Kloss (1994) suggests that students need to be "exposed to ambiguity and multiple interpretations and perspectives" (paragraph 4) in order to stimulate growth. An important part of a GSI's job is to stop the students from leaping to conclusions and to help them realize that they should delay adopting an answer. As you ask them why, let them know you want to hear varied responses to the answers. Small groups can be useful in helping students improve their abilities to express their ideas, listen to their peers, and practice seeing issues from other viewpoints.

At the end of a class session with this sort of exercise, it wouldn't hurt to tell students that this type of learning may feel new to them—particularly if you've seen them be impatient to get an answer—but that this lengthy grappling with ideas is one of the most important things they'll learn in college.

Some Major Figures in Pedagogy

Although many people have contributed to the field of pedagogy, two noted here were selected for their applicable ideas for beginning instructors. In con-

sidering your roles, or the ways that students may benefit by working together, it useful to know about John Dewey's constructivism and Lev
Vygotsky's Zone of Proximal Development.

John Dewey

John Dewey (b. 1859–d. 1952) is often referred to as the grandfather of pedagogy. In college he was exposed to the idea of evolution, which influenced
his thinking and theories because it stood in such stark contrast to the con-
temporaneous models of nature, then seen as static and set. He came to believe that people grow in knowledge when they interact with their
environment, and that learning happens through experiences and through
social interaction.[1]

John Dewey's pedagogical belief is called *constructivism*, because it centers on the idea that knowledge is constructed upon what is already known.
If students are taught with constructivism as the pedagogical foundation,
then new information cannot be delivered like a prepackaged book on a plat-
ter. Rather, students must make connections between what they are learning
and what they already know. The ramifications for teaching responsibilities
under constructivism are obviously very different than the responsibilities
assumed by the model of lecturing with occasional tests.

Lev Vygotsky

Lev Vygotsky (b. 1896–d. 1934) was a psychologist and linguist whose theories of learning hinge on social interaction. He made a useful distinction that
he described as "the distance between the actual development level as determined by independent problem solving and the level of potential development as determined through problem solving under adult guidance or in
collaboration with more capable peers" (Vygotsky, 1978, p. 86). The Zone
of Proximal Development reminds us that beyond what we know there is an
area of what we are ready to know and what we can learn—with guidance.
Teaching across that gap is called *scaffolding*, because of the way instructors

---

[1] Teachers, Dewey believed, needed to address the interests of children and nurture curiosity. Dewey
taught at universities in Michigan, Chicago (where he founded his famous laboratory school), and New
York. He, along with William James, Oliver Wendell Holmes Jr., and Charles Sanders Peirce, developed
the philosophy of pragmatism. Dewey's fame as an important thinker spread out into the wider public
mind because he wrote for popular intellectual magazines on issues such as women's suffrage and the
unionization of teachers (Festenstein, 2005).

or more knowledgeable peers can offer guidance from what is already known into what is not quite known.

Activities, such as ungraded quizzes that test students' "preknowledge" prior to delving into a new topic can be a boon in determining the boundaries of the gap that must be crossed.

Special Attention to Undergraduates

The Learning Paradigm

More than twenty years ago, Robert B. Barr and John Tagg (1995) wrote an article titled "A New Paradigm for Undergraduate Education," that appeared in *Change* and has become a touchstone for student-centered learning. The authors question many of the traditional methods of teaching used by colleges and universities by detailing the goals of the "Instruction Paradigm" and drawing up a parallel list for the "Learning Paradigm"—the former addressing the needs and the habits of the institution and the teachers, and the latter examining education from the viewpoint of the learner. Their thesis is that institutions of higher learning suffer from a range of problems, some of which could be addressed by adopting what many see as the best practice for undergraduates—student-centered instruction.

Principles of Undergraduate Education

Arthur W. Chickering and Zelda F. Gamson (1987) reviewed fifty years of research to ascertain the most effective ways to teach undergraduates. They developed a list of seven principles that lay a foundation for teaching students from all backgrounds, experiences, and skill levels. The principles, briefly, are to promote contact between students and instructors, encourage cooperation among students, promote active learning, provide prompt feedback, emphasize time on task, communicate high standards, and respect diverse talents and learning styles. The sum of advice might be described as being respectful. None of the principles are difficult to put into practice.

Bloom's Taxonomy

Benjamin Bloom developed a hierarchy of cognitive development known as *Bloom's taxonomy* (1956), which has been adopted widely in educational circles for many purposes. Bloom labeled six levels of cognition:

1. Knowledge
2. Comprehension
3. Application
4. Analysis
5. Synthesis
6. Evaluation

Simply described, Bloom believed that each level of thinking uses the previous ones in order to perform cognitive operations. We have to remember, however, and remind students from time to time, that simply having knowledge blocks does not mean we will do the next level of thinking flawlessly, nor that we will know we're missing critical knowledge blocks as we move ahead to analyze or evaluate. Thus we see people of all ages at all levels of education draw conclusions based on incomplete information.

The categories of Bloom's taxonomy have led to many lists of verbs that fall into each area—verbs that can serve you as you plan discussions or quizzes. Here is one example (Table 2.1).

Table 2.1
Bloom's Taxonomy Linked to Verbs

Knowledge	Count, Define, Describe, Draw, Find, Identify, Label, List, Match, Name, Quote, Recall, Recite, Sequence, Tell, Write
Comprehension	Conclude, Demonstrate, Discuss, Explain, Generalize, Identify, Illustrate, Interpret, Paraphrase, Predict, Report, Restate, Review, Summarize, Tell
Application	Apply, Change, Choose, Compute, Dramatize, Interview, Prepare, Produce, Role-play, Select, Show, Transfer, Use
Analysis	Analyze, Characterize, Classify, Compare, Contrast, Debate, Deduce, Diagram, Differentiate, Discriminate, Distinguish, Examine, Outline, Relate, Research, Separate
Synthesis	Compose, Construct, Create, Design, Develop, Integrate, Invent, Make, Organize, Perform, Plan, Produce, Propose, Rewrite
Evaluation	Appraise, Argue, Assess, Choose, Conclude, Critic, Decide, Evaluate, Judge, Justify, Predict, Prioritize, Prove, Rank, Rate, Select

From "Bloom's Taxonomy Verbs," http://www.teach-nology.com/worksheets/time_savers/bloom/. *Copyright 2007 by* Teachnology. Reprinted with permission.

Pedagogy of Performance

The taxonomy of Bloom and others who have built on his work is not embraced by those who focus on performance, such as nursing or dance. Rather than using conventional school products, these disciplines of practice look to aesthetic, empirical, personal, and ethical knowing. (Schoenhofer, 2007).

Making Use of Technology

The tools of teaching and learning are many, and the rule to follow is: Use any and every device and application that works for you *in service to teaching and learning.*[2]

Some GSIs feel forced into using or not using a teaching tool because it is either in vogue or passé. Do not allow yourself to be railroaded into adopting something that feels awkward for you or ignoring a tool that you are comfortable with. (On the other hand, don't avoid a technology that appeals to you simply because you don't know how to use it; workshops, tutorials, and peers are all good instructors.) Determine what best suits your course, you, and your students—whether it's podcasts of Really Simple Syndication (RSS) feeds or original documents from the special collections section of the library. Let creativity and practicality be your guides.

The challenge of technology in education is to locate those tools that will serve teaching and learning most effectively. In terms of communication—personal and group—cell phones, e-mail, and courseware fulfill many slots that were once restricted to paper and telephones. Information uses abound, from note-taking devices like Alphasmart and Treo or various types of small computers, to massive scanning of original, precious documents in order to make them widely available via the Internet. Web sites, from personal blogs to public service to the work of academics and researchers worldwide (its original intent[3]) to an unfathomable range of offerings in between offer GSIs, faculty members, and students a wealth of resources that should inspire nothing short of awe and learning.

---

[2] Tom Rocklin, associate provost for undergraduate education and the first director of the Center for Teaching at the University of Iowa, is an early adapter and high enthusiast of technological innovations, but this phrase was his wise mantra and an important part of his legacy to the center.

[3] Tim Berners-Lee of Massachusetts Institute of Technology in 1989 invented the World Wide Web, based within the Internet, as a way for information to be shared globally. The following year, he developed the first browser. For more information, see http://www.w3.org/People/Berners-Lee.

Convenience is not always the best guide to follow. Technology should serve the best practices of teaching; it should not enslave instructors or rule the way they work.

Outside Class: Cyberware

E-mail

E-mail has been mentioned in other places, but it belongs here because it has transformed communication between instructors and students. Students, who see e-mail as an extremely comfortable means of communication, are more likely to contact their faculty or GSIs with a message, while they may feel completely intimidated about coming to an office hour. Some GSIs have told me that they have had lengthy conversations about course material with students over e-mail and find it tremendously rewarding.

To help avoid misunderstandings with students, spell out how often you will check for e-mail from them and how often you expect them to check for messages from you. If they have group projects, or if you rely on them to read a mass class e-mail regarding a schedule or location change, for instance, their logging in regularly will be crucial. Many students have several accounts, so this reminder to them is important.

Courseware programs (see below) are linked to student information and allow for e-mail addresses to be "dumped" into the site you create. If you're not using courseware, require students to send you a message the first week, so you can easily create an address list for the class in your own e-mail program.

Once the logistics of e-mail are established, the only other situations to be concerned about are problems that sometimes occur within the messages themselves. A GSI once phoned me about a tiff she was having with a student on e-mail. The student had gone to a friend's wedding and missed the deadline for turning in an assignment. Instead of dealing with the student's situation, the GSI was highly annoyed by the student's informal manner and what she perceived as cockiness in the messages. She had fired back a few responses that may have made the situation worse. She forwarded the messages to me. As a neutral reader, I couldn't see any disrespect in the student's tone, but the GSI knew his voice and manner, and I didn't. She may also have been annoyed because the student knew the penalty for late assignments but hoped to skirt it. The result was unnecessary frustration and wasted time.

If you receive an e-mail that annoys you, leave it alone for a while. If you still are piqued when you return, write something such as: "You'll need to speak to me about this situation in person; please make an appointment after our next class." That will end the exchange and forestall aggravation on either side. If, for some reason, a continued exchange is necessary, and you feel uncomfortable about the messages, forward them to your supervisor for advice.

It is also a good idea to exercise caution when using humor in e-mails. Some phrases are very funny and easily understood if there is a tone of voice and facial expression to go along with them, but as words on the screen, they can look insulting. Imagine all the things the word "really" can mean, depending on inflection and expression.

If students have used e-mail only with friends and family, they may assume that it's fine to be extremely casual with you and use all sorts of coded shortcuts. The style is often informal and nonprofessional—as would be expected among friends. Some sites on the Web offer advice on "netiquette" and you may want to add a URL to your syllabus. When you e-mail students, use a tone and format that models the kind of e-mail that is appropriate between instructors and students—warm and professional.

Courseware

Courseware encompasses two types of interactive programming. One tool includes course- or discipline-specific applications. Examples include environmental science programs that illustrate earthquakes or volcanoes, online guides for tutorials in math or computer use, or any of a plethora of topics that have been developed for solo use by students or as a guide for instructors to use as they explain a phenomenon.

The other major category is course management systems. Some institutions have devised these systems for use on their own campuses, but several such systems are licensed to colleges and universities. They include, among others, Blackboard, WebCT, Web Course in a Box, Lotus LearningSpace, TopClass, and WebMentor. These programs have revolutionized many aspects of course management, providing online methods of creating a grade book (with student data "poured in" from the registrar's office) and keeping track of assessment matters, administering and grading quizzes, sending messages to all students, presenting pre- or postclass material or questions and comments, and so on. Opportunities to conduct threaded discussions that either continue conversations on topics that arise in class or the chance to discuss side issues are a major benefit for students who engage with the material and have the desire to continue talking, especially for those who are shy. The programs have become easy to master; many online tutorials exist.

A fair critique of these programs is that they can, of course, demand extra setup time initially, and attending to threaded discussions or chat rooms also absorbs time. But in many instances, this use of time is highly valuable for student learning (and may substitute for in-class assignments) or for efficient record keeping.

A hazard of the programs can be the temptation to alter the syllabus or assignments after they've been posted. Students justifiably become perturbed when professors or GSIs shift due dates or modify assignment specifications on short notice. Who can blame them? The worst case I've heard about concerned a professor who told her class in the last few weeks of a course that she would post the questions for the final exam "shortly." Two weeks after her declaration (and after several messages from harried students), the final questions were available on the Web—three days before they were due. This example is extreme, but instructors need to be careful to attend to Web upkeep in the same manner they want their students to keep up on assignments.

New GSIs or faculty members who are not familiar with courseware, who are not computer savvy, and who are not required by their department to use it during their first year might consider familiarizing themselves with it but postponing a full embrace until after experimenting a little and gaining some knowledge of it. Browse the product Web sites or attend workshops or classes offered by your information technology department.

If and when you do adopt such a program, be clear with students about

- your expectations for how often they should sign in and participate.
- the parts that are static, the parts that may change depending on the way class develops (if that is an issue), and the parts that are not completely developed.

Be sure to tell students that you are using the flexibility of the program to be able to adapt to the class's pace and to keep later alterations to a minimum—or whatever your reasons are—so that they will be better prepared for any modifications you make.

PDAs, M-Learning, Podcasting, and More

The use of personal digital assistants (PDAs) is growing in higher education. Research on the usage of PDAs is widespread in universities in the United Kingdom, New Zealand, Finland, India, and elsewhere in the world, as well as in the United States. Unsurprisingly, the disciplines that were the early adopters of the technology include business and computer science, but the use of M-learning devices has spread to many other disciplines. Well before 2000, students were using PDAs to collect data, write papers, check facts, and synchronize data with desktops and laptops (Dean, 2002).

Podcasting is one of the most recent technological developments to move into higher education; enthusiasm for its uses has even spawned the word *podogogy*. The asynchronicity of e-mail echoes in the methods used in podcasting. Audio and visual materials on the Web (including, in some cases, professors' lectures) are made available over the Internet for people to listen to or watch at their convenience. Students can download a podcast on their portable listening device and play it back at their discretion—more than once, if they choose. Two sites that may inform and inspire you are http://www.mlearningworld.com and http://www.mlearn.org.za. A browser search for "mlearning" will yield scores of other resources.

Your pedagogical style will inevitably shift as you gain experience, read about, think about, and talk about teaching with others. As you refine your skills, you will find that your own teaching practices gain depth and that your teaching philosophy matures. These elements will contribute to your developing improved methods for managing a course, engaging students, and creating a rewarding educational experience for all involved.

References

Banikowski, A. K., & Mehring, T. A. (1999, October). Strategies to enhance memory based on brain-research. *Focus on Exceptional Children, 32*. Retrieved October 10, 2006, from http://www.findarticles.com/p/articles/mi_qa3813/is_199910/ai_n 8868458

Barr, R. B., & Tagg, J. (1995, November/December). A new paradigm for undergraduate education. *Change*. Retrieved June 23, 2006, from http://critical.tamucc.edu/~blalock/readings/tch2learn.htm

Bloom, B. S., & Krathwohl, D. R. (1956). *Taxonomy of educational objectives: The classification of educational goals.* New York: Longmans, Green.

Bloom's Taxonomy Verbs. (2007). *Teachnology*. Retrieved December 1, 2006, from http://www.teach-nology.com/worksheets/time_savers/bloom/

Chickering, A. W., & Gamson, Z. F. (1987, October). Seven principles for good practice in undergraduate education. *American Association of Higher Education Bulletin*. Retrieved June 24, 2006, from http://honolulu.hawaii.edu/intranet/committees/FacDevCom/guidebk/teachtip/7princip.htm

Dean, K. (2002, November 12). Study: PDAs good for education. *Wired News*. Retrieved May 15, 2006, from http://www.wired.com/news/school/0,1383,56297,00.html?tw = wn_story_related

Dewey, J. (1916). *Democracy and education*. New York: Macmillan

Festenstein, M. (2005, February 9). Dewey's political philosophy. *Stanford Encyclopedia of Philosophy*. Retrieved September 5, 2006, from http://plato.stanford.edu/entries/dewey-political/

Kloss, R. (1994). A nudge is best helping students through the Perry Scheme of Intellectual Development [Electronic version]. *College Teaching*, *42*(4), 151–154. Retrieved October 10, 2006, from http://dhc.ucdavis.edu/fh/ct/kloss.html

Rapaport, W. J. (2006, March). William Perry's scheme of intellectual and ethical development: A journey along the 9 "Perry" positions (as modified by Belenky_et_al._1986). Retrieved October 16, 2006, from http://www.cse.buffalo.edu/~rapaport/perry.positions.html

Schoenhofer, S. (2007, January 12). Message posted in thread: Re: [POD] Taxonomies to POD@listserv.nd.edu

Scriven, M., & Paul, R. (n.d.). Defining critical thinking. *The Critical Thinking Community*. Retrieved October 15, 2006, from http://www.criticalthinking.org/aboutCT/definingCT.shtml

Vygotsky, L. S. (1978). *Mind and society: The development of higher mental processes*. Cambridge, MA: Harvard University Press.

3

THE FIRST DAY

From the beginning of the first session, virtually everything that happens in a classroom influences the dynamics of the class. Creating a friendly atmosphere where courteous and respectful behavior are the norm will set **A Tone That Signals Community** without undercutting an instructor's **Authority in the Classroom,** which is not an uncommon concern for new teachers.

Not all classrooms are ideal for every type of course, so you may have to give some attention to the **Facilities and Their Modifications** in order to make the space work best for you and your students.

A frequent question for new faculty and new GSIs centers on **Your First Class—Instruction or Only Orientation**. Despite what others do, you should decide for yourself the best way to open your course. As you anticipate the schedule of that first day, anticipate ways of **Dealing With Anxiety**, a common concern for nearly every new instructor. Regardless of your discipline or the types of instruction you will practice, when **Day One Arrives**, you will find that by **Employing Active Learning From the Start**, your expectations about high student engagement will be well communicated. As part of that engagement, be aware of **Messages to Students . . . Subtle and Bold** and the sensitivities that lay the groundwork for **Recognizing and Valuing Our Diversity**. Finally, enjoy the energy you derive from **Introducing Students to Your Discipline**, and expect to enjoy **A Great Start**.

What would you want your first class to be like? When students leave your room, what do you want them to be thinking about? How do you want them to feel about you and about this first session? Here are some practical tips and some issues to consider that can have an impact on your first day in the classroom. A well-devised plan boosts confidence and will give your students a strong sense of clarity about the way your course will run.

Before your first class:

- Make a list. You'll want to cover several items during the first session, and they may not flow from one to the other. Having a list to check off as you go along ensures that you will cover everything. It also provides a way to move from one point to another. Look at the list and say, "Let's see. What's next?" Topics to cover may include content of the course, materials—their strengths *and* their shortcomings, if any; introductions; plans for learning activities; and some university and departmental policies. Don't feel that you need to crowd all relevant information into the first session. You'll want to make time for students to speak, too.
- Prepare your opening remarks. If your anxiety is high, write out the first few sentences. This simple exercise can help ease nerves substantially.
- Find a private place—a bathroom, your car, a stairwell—and speak your first few sentences aloud, in ringing tones. It is good for you to hear yourself speak these words, and saying them loudly will help you slow down your speech and enunciate more clearly. Remember that what you plan to say is perfectly obvious to you, but your students will be hearing your words, your rhythms of speech, and your voice for the first time. You don't want them to strain to understand you.
- Review your syllabus or class guidelines, annotating or highlighting topics you expect to discuss. (See chapter 4.)
- Read and reread the list of enrolled students. Learning student names is important, and hearing or reading the name of someone before meeting that person generally speeds the process of connecting the name with the face.
- Visit your classroom(s) to see the capacity and the arrangement of desks; check audiovisual equipment, if relevant, and determine which switches turn on which lights.

A Tone That Signals Community

Consider some of your best undergraduate courses, and consider the attributes of those classes. Many of us think about instructors who were articulate, who lectured clearly, and who told captivating stories to illustrate concepts or to humanize a distant figure. We might also recall lively debates or discussions with students who were engaged, who asked good questions, or who offered provocative responses. Such classes were exciting to go to because the whole group created an intellectual excitement that inspired us in our individual thinking and understanding.

We cannot demand that such a class exist or prescribe it to our students. We have to create it, one session at a time. You accomplish this challenge in a number of ways, but the overall creation derives from your leadership. High intellectual standards and an enthusiastic belief in your subject and your students will set the stage for a successful course. Strategies, methods, activities, and other details in the chapters on discussions and assignments may serve you well, but your attitudes about your students and the course materials will be a major force in the classroom.

The notion of creating a community of learners has become a common way of discussing goals for college classrooms.[1] Many of the attributes of a nurturing community can be replicated in a classroom, including becoming acquainted with one another and developing a mutuality of providing assistance and exhibiting respect. This model of a classroom runs against the stereotyped portrait of the stern professor lecturing to—and at the same time ignoring—students. Since all of us have been members of communities, we know the hallmarks of some of the best ones and can use these community practices even if they seem unexpected in a class. For instance, the late Chris Christiansen, of Harvard University, shook hands with his students as they entered the room and introduced himself to each one (Derek Bok Center for Teaching and Learning, 1995). Students do not expect this behavior in a classroom, but I have tried it and found it to be highly effective. Such a greeting made a palpable difference in how soon the class began to feel like a community, and the brief face-to-face encounter helped me learn names more quickly, too.

Begin creating your community on the first day.

Authority in the Classroom

By virtue of being a faculty member, GSI, mentor, grader, monitor, or consultant, you wear the cloak of authority as surely as the conch was used to

---

[1] A great deal has been written about the notion of a community of learners in college classrooms. Seminal and inspirational works include those by John Dewey (1916), Patricia Cross (1998), and an article by Robert B. Barr and John Tagg (1995), which is described in chapter 2.

signal who had the right to speak in the troop of marooned boys in William Golding's novel *Lord of the Flies*. You are the one who separates the correct answers from the incorrect answers, and you recognize well-developed arguments as opposed to the hastily assembled seat-of-the-pants offerings. You understand the syllabus, and in many cases you are the one who gives grades.

Some new instructors put authority and friendliness on the same continuum but at opposite ends. However they are not opposites, because they are not on the same continuum. Faculty members and GSIs can exercise the authority that their position grants them and still behave in a friendly manner.

New GSIs, especially, may want to err on the "friendly" side because they fear being seen as autocratic. In most cases, it is beneficial for students to understand the boundary between you and them. Students who don't sense the border are more likely to assume they can cross it, for instance, by requesting extensions for due dates, pestering you about points taken off in quizzes or examinations, expecting you to extend extraordinary understanding for absences or tardiness, contacting you at inappropriate times, and so on. Each of these situations might be legitimate in isolated cases, but any experienced faculty member or GSI who has had a student or two cross the boundary over and over will tell you that dealing with these requests occupies too much time and energy.

GSIs and new faculty create a persona of authority by being confident and clear about standards and expectations and in their explanations of assignments, tests, and so on. The tone and detail of your syllabus or class guidelines also build your authority. Respecting students, helping them through disagreements, and addressing course material in a scholarly manner also foster classroom authority. All of these things can be done with warmth and friendliness; none of them demands a mandatory distance.

Gender also plays a part in authority. Because of the role of the patriarchy historically, men in many fields—from news anchors to doctors to judges—are viewed as more authoritative before they've even opened their mouths. Many more female instructors report student behavior that mimics the comfort students have with their mothers, such as being whined to for special treatment. Reports surface periodically about the role of gender in the classroom, as evidenced by student evaluations that say women teachers are seen as less effective if they look young, if they are small, if they are nonwhite, or if they are international GSIs. Ironically, female faculty and GSIs may be evaluated more poorly if they don't supply the sort of nurturing that students expect from women, while male instructors gain extra credit for exercising this feminine attribute. Women have also been criticized for teaching while pregnant. Some female GSIs or faculty may face every one of the obstacles noted above. As more women become presidents of major universities and gain more leadership roles in government, these attitudes may continue to diminish, but who knows if they will ever disappear?

Young male GSIs and faculty may also encounter students who assume the teacher will do what their same-age pals would do—excuse an absence, allow late assignments, laugh off an inappropriate comment during class, and so on. The fact is that college instructors do not expect to have to deal with requests or actions that cross the line, but sometimes these things occur. The foreknowledge that it might happen will reduce a sense of surprise if such behaviors occur and will help you prepare your responses.

Introductions and Appearance

Instructors can make wardrobe choices that contribute to an air of authority. I always regret making this point, because we would like to think that the cover of the book doesn't matter, but realistically, in the United States at least, appearance has an effect. Our initial reactions to clothing, hair, jewelry, and other such matters influence our first opinions of people. We have all had the experience of having those reactions altered dramatically after we begin speaking with the person, but the fact is that wardrobe stereotypes are used by viewers to assess how people define themselves. And we each exercise wardrobe and other choices to adopt a public persona in order to fit into a group or make a statement in opposition to a group.

The media's portrayal of a male professor has long included a slightly shabby tweed jacket with leather elbow patches. This "uniform" has been connected to academics for decades and will probably continue, even if moderated, for years to come. In any event, you can send some classic signals of authority to your class by wearing a jacket. Some GSIs and new faculty avoid jeans, at least initially. I've heard GSIs say to female peers that they should add appropriate jewelry. A final note on wardrobe would be that discipline matters. Instructors in finance, for example, reside in a different world of expectations and society than GSIs in theater. Regardless of the department, observe how senior faculty dress (male, female, older, younger), and look at the students' wardrobes. The differences may not be vast, but by following the established model, you will find yourself being treated more like a professor.

First Name, Last Name

Another decision to make for the classroom concerns how you would like to be addressed, which is another detail that can affect authority. Some students may take it for granted that they can call you by your given name, and others—especially those from countries outside the United States—will be uncomfortable with that level of informality. In some disciplines and some institutions, both professors and students use only last names. Do what feels appropriate and comfortable. It is perfectly legitimate to offer your last name only; you can offer your first name later to individuals or to the whole class.

Remember, no attributes of wardrobe or address prevent you from being friendly to students by, for example, laughing and chatting about campus news or other appropriate topics. Students from the United States, particularly, expect friendliness in their instructors. Nevertheless, you can make choices to establish and preserve both authority and appropriate boundaries.

Facilities and Their Modifications

Lights, air, desks or tables, and chairs. These aspects of a classroom sum up the usual elements that define classroom space. Secondary characteristics may include location and sounds. Do what you can to make the room serve you and your students.

In many classrooms, especially older ones, you cannot do a great deal with the lights—they are on or they are off, sufficient or insufficient. Maybe they're full-spectrum bulbs, which many people prefer, rather than fluorescent ones. Perhaps you have big windows or none at all. Unless you need a darkened room for media presentations, make the room as bright as possible. Students will be able to see the board and their notes better.

Unless you're teaching a lab or in a studio setting, move free-standing desks, with the help of students, into a circle or arc so they can see one another face to face. If they are seated face to back, they will unsurprisingly behave more like an audience, and many of them will be less likely to speak up.

When a room is too cold, too hot, or stuffy, you may be able to open a window, but lots of classroom buildings have sealed windows. Speak to your department secretary or call the office in charge of classrooms to ask if anything can be done. If you and your students are fated to spend the term in a difficult room, exercise empathy. Give students a thirty-second hallway break—or at least a stand-and-stretch—halfway through class. Be strict about the time or it will turn into a five-minute bathroom and cell phone break; it would be best to lead them out and guide them back in the first few times.

Your First Class—Instruction or Only Orientation

On many campuses, a widely held assumption about the first day is that it contains two activities:

- Taking roll
- Reviewing the syllabus

These events can indeed fulfill responsibilities and requirements. Some instructors even defend the idea of not teaching during the first class or even the second or the third, because students are in the "shop-and-drop" mode.

The practice of shop and drop—students sitting in on or signing up for more courses than they will eventually take in order to see which classes and which teachers they want—has become so common on some campuses that it's an expected part of a school year. Consequently some teachers wait a few days before beginning the actual work of the course. At Texas Christian University, the administration has fought back. The registrar instituted a policy that bars students from signing up for eighteen or more credits before classes begin. This plan prevents students from essentially reserving space in more classes than they will take and discourages browsing for courses the way they might for a DVD player. It also encourages teachers to begin teaching on the first day (Parker, 2004). You will no doubt quickly learn about the customs on your own campus.

A strong case can be made for beginning your course when the students enter the classroom.

- The contracted course has begun. As part of upholding high standards, you have the right to assume that students are there to begin their studies. Some students drive long distances, hire babysitters, and arrange work schedules in order to attend class. Why should they be given some handouts and dismissed after ten minutes?

- Most instructors have more course material to teach than will fit into a term, regardless of its length. Postponing the opportunity to begin does not make good sense.
- For those students who are shopping or sitting in without being registered, your behavior will let them know the expectations you have for students. For some, it may be precisely what they are looking for; for others, it will be precisely what they want to avoid.
- Consider tape-recording your first few classes. Students who miss them can borrow the tapes; this taping keeps you from having to re-teach the class again and again.

I would not want to leave the impression that you should present yourself as a stern, no-nonsense instructor with nothing but lesson plans on your mind. Teaching and learning certainly entail hard work, but the truth is that they are exciting and fun. The first day has the potential to signal a great deal to your students, including

- your enthusiasm for the course and your students
- the pleasures of participation, even on the nerve-jangling first day
- the tone and mood you set for the class
- the high standards that will be expected

Consider how we all develop opinions about situations and people within the first hour of contact. Many of the impressions do not even register on a conscious level, but we carry away a lot of feelings about a relationship from that first meeting. Why not make the most of it?

Dealing With Anxiety

Rare is the new faculty member or GSI who does not feel anxiety about this new undertaking. Such feelings are completely normal. Ignore people who say you should not be nervous or that you have nothing to be nervous about. Such palliatives are not true, and deciding not to be nervous is a bit like deciding not to be awake.

Accept your nervousness, but keep in mind the fact that it will diminish.

For most instructors, anxiety shrinks enormously after the first two classes. By then you will have had time to actually *be* a teacher in the sense that you will have begun to know and interact with students, to understand how the dynamics of the class are developing, and to behave and be treated like an instructor.

Day One Arrives

Come to class five minutes early. The benefits of this small act can be enormous. As a practical matter, you can adjust lighting and desks or chairs; you can also unpack books and papers and spread them out for good access. You may have media equipment to set up, too. More important, arriving early gives you time to greet students and engage in some small talk. Continue this custom as the term passes. Students will come to rely on your availability and use it to ask questions or to arrange an appointment for another time.

Students appreciate—and rate—teachers highly for being accessible (Gall, Knight, Carlson, & Sullivan, 2003).[2] Adopting a custom that makes you regularly available communicates to students that you are there to help them. I recall an experienced GSI telling me that his classes that term seemed somehow out of sync. He couldn't figure out how to perk things up. I suggested he try arriving early for class. Though he was midway through the semester, he initiated the practice immediately. At the end of the course, he told me that the change completely shifted the tone of both classes. He said that the effect was so positive that he planned to adopt the practice as a permanent part of his teaching.

Although the thought of arriving early on the first day may cause you jitters, the alternative—walking into the room at the moment class is to begin—raises another specter: students seated, unpacked and waiting, eyes aimed at you, and you, under their curious gaze, unpacking your things, trying to put things in order and introduce the course simultaneously, while all the time conveying confidence, competence, and warmth. No small challenge. Early in my teaching, I arrived on time once, began unloading my armful of papers, and immediately sent stacks of handouts cascading across

---

[2] The study looked at 181 courses, and students overwhelmingly rated accessibility issues such as feeling connected to the instructor, receiving feedback from him or her, and appreciating the availability to answer questions between 90 and 98 percent, regardless of the expected grade or the workload of the course.

the desk and onto the floor. It was one of those moments in life that I wished had been fantasy instead of reality. At the end of the course, I received more than a few evaluations that began, "She seemed disorganized initially, but once the class got going, things went well." I was glad I could redeem myself, but no one needs to make a first impression like that one.

Employing Active Learning From the Start

Regardless of discipline, your first session can convey expectations to students about the culture of the class and provide experiences that indicate the sorts of classroom behaviors that you hope to nurture.

Whether in the humanities or the sciences, discussion classes of one sort or another are the most common courses assigned to GSIs. Running effective discussion sections has many challenges, but a major one is finding ways to persuade students to participate, to speak up. This is not surprising since students carry the same apprehensions about public speaking as everyone else. If they have to speak, they want to appear smart and articulate. While a few of your students will probably be eager participators, most will not.

Taking Roll

The easiest way for any of us to speak comfortably among strangers is to discuss something we know about and have discussed in the past. Take advantage of this common trait by altering the way you take roll. People are accustomed to answering "Here"—familiar and brief—and nothing else. After they declare their presence, ask a question about their hometown, dorm life, apartment, or about food facilities, parking spaces, weather, or other factors appropriate to your campus or location. This little spontaneous public-speaking exercise will help students begin to relax. Some students will be funny, which will add to the comfort in the class. Asking an undemanding follow-up question serves three purposes.

1. Every student will hear his or her voice in that classroom among that group of people; a familiarity begins to develop that fosters a friendly atmosphere.
2. You will have the relief of having eyes off you for several moments, and students will react to each other, not just to you. This benefit is

not to be underestimated; it is an enormous aid for managing stage fright.

3. Listening to your students speak while making eye contact with them initiates a sense of community and helps you begin to learn their names.

Another important opportunity in taking roll is not only to ask about nicknames but also to get help with pronunciation. You will very likely have international students in your class—or your name may be a challenge to some or all of the students. Ask two, three, or four times, if needed, whether you are pronouncing difficult names correctly. This should not be seen as an embarrassing moment. You are, in fact, conveying your intention to treat all students fairly, and in a small way you are demonstrating that you are eager to learn what you don't know. I've had students and associates from Korea, Argentina, Macedonia, Greece, and other lands whose languages were unfamiliar to me. Sometimes I asked about name pronunciations several times during the first few weeks of meeting these people. I found them to be patient with me and pleased with my determination. Likewise, people often pronounce my name as LY-berg, when LEE-berg is the correct way; I appreciate it when someone bothers to ask and then to learn the correct pronunciation.

While students are answering your questions, write down a word or two about their appearance; these clues will help you match names with faces in subsequent sessions.

Taking roll in this manner may take twenty minutes, but the purposes fulfilled make the time well spent.

Small Groups

If you plan to use small groups in your class, model them on the first or second day. Although there are several things to know about using groups effectively, which are discussed in chapter 11, an early introduction to the activity can be brief, casual, and effective. Ask students to turn to each other in groups of three or four people and address a question, such as, How would you define anthropology? American studies? Cultural geography? Or, list everything you know about imaginary numbers, the Atlantic Ocean, or Shinto.

Urging students to express their thoughts on a topic in a situation where it is clear that you are not expecting a *right* answer helps them to relax about your specific directive and also teaches them something about your approach to teaching and learning. This initial exercise allows them to gain insights into one another's thinking and personality. It can set a tone of investigation and respect. You, meanwhile, will learn about your students, what they know, how they express it, perhaps why they think what they do, and how they differ. You'll also be able to observe which students speak up easily and which seem too shy to express themselves, even in small groups.

A key tactic in using groups effectively is to interrupt them before they stop talking. It is counterintuitive, but when groups reach a point where no one has anything to say, discomfort and awkwardness set in quickly, and the experience begins to feel negative where two minutes earlier it seemed very energizing. Stop them while they are still actively talking.

Asking groups to "report out" is the last phase of the activity. Commonly, an assertive group member will volunteer to state what the group determined. This technique is fine, though others will be discussed later. Sometimes teachers write student comments on the board during the reporting out. An alternative is to ask a student to write notes on the board so you can give more attention and more eye contact to the group members.

Introductions

Finally comes the topic of introductions. Many teachers ask students to introduce themselves in some fashion during the first or second class—or both. Rather than having students give a straight introduction of themselves, you might do one of the following:

- Pair students, have them interview each other for a few minutes and then introduce one another to the rest of the group.
- Ask students to introduce themselves to a small group, and drift around the room so that you can "meet" students by eavesdropping and interrupting now and then. After a few minutes, ask each member of the group to introduce one other person giving one detail learned about that person.

Requiring students to speak in a fairly low-risk setting during the first two or three classes will go a long way toward establishing a congenial atmosphere and boosting participation in class.

If the day comes when you teach a class of one, two, or three hundred students, begin class with this same routine. If groups of four, five, or six students introduce themselves for a few minutes, the exchange will lend some community to the session and counteract the sense of alienation that big classes unwittingly promote.

Icebreakers

If you want some adventurous methods for helping people become comfortable or ways to learn names, listen to experienced GSIs or faculty members.

Some instructors use icebreakers the first day, while others wait for the second session. The classic "Two Truths and a Lie," which is often used to learn names and personalities ("I'll tell you three things about me, but only two are true. Guess which one's a lie.") can be modified in any number of ways to adapt to college. In a class where students may be writing personal essays, the version of "two things you can tell by looking at me and one that you can't" can be referred to later by teachers in discussing how writers craft their method of revealing information in essays. In a geography section, you might ask about two places students have been and one they haven't been (or wouldn't want to go). History courses could use events, and many disciplines could use public figures in the field—two people I'd like to have dinner with and one I would not. You can also ask open-ended questions, such as, "Why are you taking this class?" or "What is your background in a particular discipline or topic?" If you don't attach the questions to roll taking, be sure to have people say their names before they give their comments.

A lot of the nervousness evident in the first session will be diminished by the next class, which will make conversation easier. By the end of the second session, students will have spoken twice—a big help for coming discussions or their willingness to ask questions.

Messages to Students . . . Subtle and Bold

Mandatory Information

Your university and department will prescribe points of information that students must be given during the first class—verbally and/or in the syllabus. Topics may include policies on attendance, plagiarism, formal complaints, grading, the management of class materials (for science laboratories, art classes), and so on.

Students quickly learn to expect a litany of such details because that is often the way classes begin, but if the information is in a handout, you can devote only the briefest time to it in the first class, perhaps returning to it the next class after students have read it. Because a lot of the policies have to do with penalties linked to unethical or illegal behavior, plan how you will discuss them. I have heard of instructors who, during their first session, describe the consequences of inappropriate student behavior with such Dickensian harshness that students felt as if they were being reprimanded for things they hadn't done—not a good way to begin a class when the goal is to promote a sense of community.

Although you must present some serious and perhaps harsh information, discuss the course itself first and last so that your enthusiasm and the connections you make with your students will create the dominant impressions of the day.

Office Hours

Most institutions require faculty and GSIs who teach to hold office hours. Try to select both early and late hours, and choose days that run against typical class session schedules. An office hour right after class is better than one right before; the latter may be handy for students, but sometimes you will want that hour for yourself. Be sure to tell students where your office is located. Freshmen new to large campuses are often befuddled by the host of buildings.

Use the description of office hours to talk about your eagerness to meet with students, the value of conferences, and your willingness to arrange appointments at other times. (You may think this offer will cause a deluge that overwhelms your schedule, but unless conferences are required, very few students, unfortunately, seek them.)

Contact Information

As described in "Constructing a Syllabus," in chapter 4, p. 50, you will want to give students office and department telephone numbers and your supervisor's information if you're a GSI. The location of the department should be included, too, if there is a possibility students would drop off assignments there for your mailbox.

When you give out your e-mail address (or an address for an account you create specifically for students), tell students how long they should expect to wait for a response, since some students will expect an answer almost instantly. I knew a playwright GSI in a theater department who needed to quarantine himself to work on writing his plays. He quickly realized he had to limit e-mails in order to do his own work, so his students adapted to his schedule, which was that he would respond to e-mails from 5:00 p.m. to 6:00 p.m. on Wednesdays and 6:00 p.m. to 8:00 p.m. on Thursdays. If the time slots did not work for the students, they needed to telephone him or go to his office.

Some teachers give out home and cell telephone numbers to everyone and some do not. If you give them out, tell students the hours you can be called, whether you will accept text messages (surcharges are part of some telephone plans), and so on. I once read about a GSI in a math department who said he did not mind being contacted any time—if students were puzzled by a problem at 2:00 a.m. and called him, he was happy to help. That sort of availability is remarkable but certainly not a standard expectation.

The fact is that most students will not abuse your contact information; they will appreciate your making yourself available to them. This aspect of your teaching persona conveys an availability that students value (Gall et al., 2003).

Body Language

While many characteristics create a demeanor, the most important habits to develop are to look at your students and to smile occasionally. Eye contact in the United States usually translates into sincerity and honesty. If you have grown up in a nation or culture where eye contact is avoided, this behavior may be a challenge for you initially. Express friendliness in other ways until eye contact becomes comfortable; your students will respond accordingly.

Your actions will make a difference, too. Some teachers remain behind a built-in console where they manage PowerPoint slides and Web sites. New teachers may feel more comfortable standing or sitting behind a desk, but make an effort to eliminate objects between your students and you—at least part of the time. Pull your chair to the side of the desk for a while. If the room layout allows mingling, walk among students a few times.

How You Speak

It is so obvious to state that teachers need to speak clearly and to express themselves well that you may think this section is superfluous. For some people, it may be, but instruction in public speaking has been on the decline in the United States for decades, and a few tips from people who attend to performance issues in the classroom may be helpful to you.

You should assume that your pronunciation of English will not be entirely clear to everyone in the room. Even if all of your students are from the United States and you are, too, some students may have grown up in an area where the accent differs from yours. You may have students with partial hearing loss. And you very likely will, in fact, have students from other countries. Watch student facial expressions; they will tell you a lot about whether you are being understood.

Another common speaking habit is talking quickly and "swallowing" the ends of words or sentences. Your students will lose part of what you are saying and spend their time trying to understand the sounds rather than paying attention to your statements.

Rehearse. If you have a tape recorder or if you can record into your computer, stand across the room and record yourself for a few minutes. When you listen, pay attention to what stands out and what you struggle to hear.

Finally, the old tips from performers—and from many a mother—still hold: Take a deep breath and stand up straight.

Specialized Vocabulary—The Jargon of the Educated

Vocabulary is another issue to consider. As a specialist in your discipline (even if you are not too far down the path of specialization), you have become very familiar with a repertoire of jargon. These words were once unfamiliar to you—or at least their particularized usage was unfamiliar; your students are now the ones confronting the expanding and specialized vocabulary.

If you tell students that as a class you will be interpreting literature, historical documents, geological data, or a line of music, you have a specific idea in mind about what you mean by "interpret," but will they share your concept? Most high school students have a vague idea of what interpretation is—either a translation from another language, a way of playing a piece of music, or, perhaps most common, an opinion about something. To academics, the word *interpretation* means a great deal more than having an opinion. As you prepare your remarks for the first session, make a list of words that you may want to discuss. Continue this practice throughout the semester. (See chapter 10, pp. 132–135, for assignment ideas to engage your students in vocabulary issues.)

College students commonly gain thousands of new vocabulary words during their undergraduate years. In order to make the acquisition as effective as possible, discuss vocabulary both specifically and generally.

Diversity, Diversity, Diversity

All faculty members and GSIs should expect to have a diverse class of students, just as the population of instructors is diverse. While it may be obvious to you that people can get along best by being respectful and by not allowing behavior to be dictated by assumptions, teachers have the responsibility of bringing that sensibility into the classroom and setting the tone where students, too, can grow in wisdom about moving the world toward a more civilized state.

Many teaching strategies in this book contain an implied goal of inclusiveness. We want all students to learn, to participate, to find ways to manage information, to lose fears about the challenges of tackling difficult material, to feel safe enough in the classroom to express opinions that may be unpopular, to venture into their instructors' office with questions or misgivings or concerns, and so on. Wanting success for all students means being open and available to each of them, engaging each in conversation, and calling on everyone in the class. It means holding equally high expectations and extending personal sensitivity to all students—regardless of the stereotypes that their appearances may suggest. Just because a woman is obviously pregnant doesn't mean she wants to talk about babies. Just because a youth's jeans' crotch is parallel to his knees doesn't mean he's rude to adults. Just because a person's skin is a particular hue doesn't mean he or she was raised in a broken, strict, or tight-knit family. The only assumption that seems appropriate in the United States is that those from northern European backgrounds have been the majority, with the many privileges that go along with that heritage. But it does not mean that as individuals they haven't had to deal with family members with financial or alcoholic problems or with abusive relationships.

A lot needs to be "left at the door" when you teach, and you have to nurture the classroom dynamics to reinforce the safety of the classroom for all. Your being explicitly inclusive will be a strong sign to students, and it will make way for a crucial part of the learning that takes place in your classroom, whether or not it's expressed in the syllabus.

By practicing respect for individuals and operating with the belief that everyone is gathered to focus on the course at hand, no formulas are needed. You and your students will fit into every category imaginable—from needing assistive technology to feeling apprehensive about fitting in on the campus, from being a minority race/religion/gender/sexual preference/age/ethnic group (on the campus or simply in the class) to being overweight or shy, tall, or short.

We humans carry many attributes, some of which are linked to historical or current discrimination. Creating a community of learners in the classroom will be a compelling way to send the message to students that the life of the mind can be richly rewarding and that intense discussions can occur regardless of personal biases or backgrounds. Becoming more educated—formally and informally—about our diverse humanity is obviously crucial to becoming an educated person and the kind of global citizen that the world desperately needs. Do talk about diversity as part of the campus and part of life, and take appropriate opportunities to help your students become educated and seek to continue that education beyond the classroom.

Apply good practices by using a variety of teaching strategies that may vary in effectiveness for students and their learning style preferences. Welcome their questions and concerns in class and in private. These actions and your teaching behavior will provide powerful lessons and examples.

Introducing Students to Your Discipline

Some students arrive at college knowing precisely what their major will be, others come with some confidence on the matter, and still others arrive with no clear plans at all. "Undecided" is a very common answer to "What is your major?" Fifty to seventy-five percent of students change majors at least once during college (Minnesota State University Moorhead, 2006). These statistical matters are of great interest to department chairs and deans because the number of students enrolled in a department determines the number of faculty and the number of GSIs. If a department's number of students diminishes, teaching positions disappear. Over time ongoing losses can mean that a department is eliminated. Faculty are made well aware of these matters. GSIs, too, may receive a lecture on this aspect of retention, especially if their department is small.

Fiscal issues aside, both faculty and GSIs ought to introduce students to the large picture of a discipline. Questions to explore might include: How did your discipline begin? Why? Was it part of another discipline? What contributions does it make to practical life or to scholarly thinking? How has the field changed over the decades or centuries of its existence, and what influences have contributed to these changes? In other words, give a rationale—and invite students into the conversation—for your discipline and for your course within the discipline. Addressing the how and why of a field of study can set students' minds to probing thoughts they often don't bother with. Discussions about these topics during the first or second class can be an engaging way to embark on a course and to raise student enthusiasm. If retention or a growth in majors is a long-term side effect, so much the better.

The Great Start—Yours

Teaching is a complex enterprise, but by the time you have earned a degree or two and entered or reentered graduate school or completed your terminal degree, you have a great many experiences to draw from. The practical ones include all the schooling you yourself have had, all the ways you have participated in organizations or in employment positions you have held, your memories and reflections about people who were extraordinary teachers—in and out of the classroom—and the impressions you carry of people who taught badly, either through ineptness or, sadly, antipathy to students. Most of us have witnessed teaching in many forms. All of it provides background that we use in shaping our own teaching.

In his book *Advice for New Faculty Members: Nihil Nimus*, Robert Boice (2000) passes along wisdom from faculty members who had taught from four to seven years and who were invited to think about what they would have done differently if they were beginning again. Their four tips indicate how important it is for instructors to "hit the ground running" (p. 220). They would have more actively pursued social networks, sought ways "to admire and enjoy their colleagues" (p. 220), they would have assumed that students accepted them, and they would have pursued professional activities from off campus, including consulting, reviewing, and presentations. Each item would be something presumed to be part of an academic's life, and the first three are relevant for GSIs, too.

If you arrive on campus with apprehensions, which seems likely to some extent, remember that you have been hired or admitted because the institution is enthusiastic about you and your future. The administrators intend for you to thrive, to have a successful career, and to create a mutually satisfying relationship between the institution and yourself. This thought may help diminish some of the fretting or self-doubt that can come from establishing yourself in a new position in a strange place.

So your undertaking begins. Everyone who faces a new teaching position wonders and hopes and is perhaps vexed by various thoughts. It is inevitable that such a grand endeavor would give pause to an intelligent person. This thoughtfulness and reflection are precisely the qualities that make a good teacher. Guiding students along the way to their own futures will, in all likelihood, be an experience that is highly satisfying—even exhilarating. Expect to enjoy yourself.

References

Barr, R. B., & Tagg, J. (1995, November/December). A new paradigm for undergraduate education. *Change.* Retrieved June 23, 2006, from http://critical.tamucc.edu/~blalock/readings/tch2learn.htm

Boice, R. (2000) *Advice for new faculty members: Nihil nimus.* Needham Heights, MA: Allyn and Bacon.

Cross, K. P. (1998). Why learning communities? Why now? *About Campus, 3*(3), 4–11.

Derek Bok Center for Teaching and Learning, Harvard University. (Producer). (1995). *The art of discussion leading: A class with Chris Christensen* [Videotape]. (Available from the Derek Bok Center for Teaching and Learning, Harvard University, Science Center 318, One Oxford Street, Cambridge, MA 02138–2901)

Gall, K. A., Knight, D. W., Carlson, L. E., & Sullivan, J. F. (2003, October). Making the grade with students: The case for accessibility. *Journal of Engineering Education, 92*(4), pp. 337–343.

Minnesota State University Moorehead. (2006). Major? Option? Emphasis? Oh, my! Retrieved January 1, 2007, from http://www.mnstate.edu/recruitment/majors_intro.cfm

Parker, E. (2004, January 13). TCU restricting "shop and drops." *Texas Christian University Daily Skiff.* Retrieved August 1, 2006, from http://www.skiff.tcu.edu/2004/spring/issues/01/13/tcu.html

4

CREATING A SYLLABUS

In order to create a syllabus, instructors must command the full view of a course and decide on many of the details. The first question for GSIs to consider is **Syllabus or Course Guidelines— Which Works for You?** Both GSIs and new faculty will benefit from thinking about content in terms of **Your Course's "Clock."** Finally come the many elements to include when **Constructing a Syllabus**, which include, among other things, information about how and when to contact you; descriptions of the course, its goals, and learning outcomes; due dates for assignments and exams; policies for grading, plagiarism, and attendance; and expectations for classroom dynamics. The format, tone, and choice of labels also need to be considered.

The structure and the amount of detail in a syllabus depend upon several factors, including discipline, type of course, and the instructor's level of responsibility for the class. This chapter describes some issues for instructors to consider as well as several topics that should or could be part of a syllabus or class guidelines.

Syllabus or Course Guidelines—Which Works for You?

In some European countries, university classes don't have syllabi (students watch for postings on bulletin boards to see when lectures will be offered), but in the United States, students not only expect to get a syllabus, schools generally require it.

GSI responsibilities, as we have noted, lie along something that resembles a continuum in terms of student contact, control over content, and size and timing of class meetings. If you run sections for a professor whose syllabus manages the course you may be told by the professor or other GSIs that you don't need to give the students any handouts about your sessions. I would advise otherwise and strongly suggest you prepare a sheet of guidelines. New faculty and GSIs given complete responsibility for a course obviously need to create a syllabus. Before describing the two documents, here are two anecdotes.

I worked with a GSI once whose course professor told his large lecture class that he didn't care whether the students went to their sectional discussions.

Another time, I spoke with an undergraduate student who said that when everyone arrived for her discussion section, the GSI would ask if anyone had any questions from the lecture. If no one asked a question, he told the students class was over and everyone left.

In the first case, the GSI was very frustrated that the professor put so little value on the discussion section. The GSI wanted to hold a "real" class, but once the professor had spoken, his words set the tone and few students bothered to show up. I suggested that the GSI contact students by e-mail or telephone to discuss the learning activities that he'd planned and urge them to attend. Students don't expect personal contact from a new teacher with such an invitation.

In the second instance, the GSI fell down on the job. GSIs are hired to facilitate student learning, and simply asking students if they have questions, hearing nothing, and dismissing them leaves students in the lurch. Do they already know everything? It's doubtful that they do. If you are reading this book, you are not going to be one of those GSIs, but you will probably hear about them, and you will hear jealous comments about the income they receive for their little work. One has to be philosophical about these things: Slackers exist in every field.

The following section highlights the elements that belong in a syllabus, so it contains an excess of information for those preparing guidelines. Regardless of your first semester's responsibilities, you may find value in browsing through all the topics since some of them may be important for your sessions earlier than you expected.

Your Course's "Clock"

As a prelude to planning a syllabus, one consideration is the rhythm of the course itself, regardless of how long it lasts. Donna Killian Duffy and Janet

Wright Jones (1995) wrote a thoughtful book called *Teaching Within the Rhythms of the Semester* that offers instructors some provocative ideas for planning courses. The authors suggest that instructors could plan courses more effectively by paying attention to a rhythm they describe as including the initial honeymoon period of high energy, the middling period when momentum may flag, and the period of closure.

How can you make the most of these times?

Initial Energy

There is little doubt that the fall semester, more than any other I believe, begins with high hopes. Students examine their new books and resolve to do the readings in a timely fashion. They believe they will do all of their assignments neatly and thoroughly. They plan to attend every class and take good notes. Essentially, they begin by wanting to complete all assignments and earn excellent grades.

Faculty and GSIs begin the year with a lot of energy, too. The balance of research and studies and teaching seems manageable; others seem to do it successfully with no apparent complications. The challenge looks like a sturdy hike up a fairly friendly mountain, not the pitched and risky trek up a craggy alp that may fill some of the rumor mills.

If you have control over the assignments you give—and this is a large *if* for most GSIs—take advantage of all the fall resolutions and optimism by "front loading" the work. By this I mean, assign difficult readings and long papers in the first half of the course—the first third is even better. Make use of your students' good intentions in every way you can and of your own discretionary time, too, while it is still available. Many instructors cannot see a way to do this. The most common reply is that they can't assign a paper that will be due early in the term because the students don't know enough about the topic to do the work.

Let's consider the ramifications of this notion. On the surface, it seems logical. How grand it is to imagine that students will process the information in two-thirds of the course and bring their knowledge to bear on a complex topic that they will skillfully analyze and then use it to write a brilliant paper. It *can* happen, and it *does*. But the reality is that since this customary thinking propels the structure of many syllabus schedules, students end up with two, three, or four large projects or papers due in the final weeks of school. While students may possess the knowledge to do more comprehensive work by the end of the term, only the most mentally agile who need the least sleep, who don't procrastinate, and who have virtually no life outside school might successfully research and prepare that number of big projects in a two- to three-week period—and come out of it with a sense of gained knowledge or reflection on the subjects or the process. Some students may likely be preparing for examinations, too.

Therefore, develop creative assignments with unconventional due dates. These, too, can help students achieve course goals. Unconventional projects may be appropriate, too. See chapter 9 for some ideas.

Middling Energy

The middle of the course may last four to seven weeks depending on how your institution structures terms—or less for summer or special sections. More indicative of the phase than passing weeks may be the expressions on your students' faces. They may look tired and stressed and be sloppier in their assignments, late to class, or half prepared for discussion.

While no miracle cures exist for this state of listlessness, you may want to plan novel activities or experiment with less-common teaching strategies to revitalize students and pull them out of their sense of feeling overwhelmed or school weary. A field trip can be effective and so might a guest speaker. Instigating a spontaneous debate or giving an ungraded quiz, as described in chapter 8, will add spice to sessions and help reenergize students.

Closure

Classes generally end with a test and an evaluation. These items are typically mandated and out of your control. You might consider giving students a postcourse assessment tool or invite students to reflect on the course. Another plan would be a well-devised small-group extravaganza to review course goals and summarize the big picture of your course. Chapter 11 describes methods for using groups effectively.

Constructing a Syllabus

A syllabus typically contains a calendar of class meetings and the assignments that are attached to those dates. The basic model may be available in a few disciplines or for a few professors, but in recent years many more features have been added to that design.[1] Commonly expected categories include

- labels
- format and tone
- contact information
- course description
- course goals and learning outcomes
- calendar of assignments and exams
- grading proportions and policies
- assignment information
- uses of technology
- libraries and other campus resources
- attendance policy
- assistance for students with disabilities
- expectations for classroom decorum
- complaints—protocols for problems
- ethics (including plagiarism)

In addition, your institution or department will probably require information on such matters as human rights, grievance procedures, and details on campus policies.

An epigraph can be a powerful way to personalize the syllabus and put a lens on the course. Some GSIs or faculty members use a quotation from one of the course texts, and others use a personal, favorite quote to call students into the community the instructor wants to create.

Finally, you may wish to add elements that help students understand more about your discipline or about learning in college. Some instructors include advice gleaned from their teaching experiences. I had a student who was unhappy with a grade on a writing assignment because, despite the clear guidelines she'd been given, she followed an old pattern of writing she'd learned in high school. She argued her case by saying, "I've always been taught to . . ." Her comments reminded me to include remarks in the class guidelines about the new or expanded ways students will learn content and

---

[1] Judith Grunert's (1997) book, *The Course Syllabus: A Learning-Centered Approach*, addresses in detail the construction of a learner-centered syllabus.

process. In the first year of teaching and in subsequent courses, you will understand more and more about the strengths and challenges your students face as you observe how they comprehend material and where they have problems.

You may wish to include resources for students, from note-taking techniques to suggestions for improving academic writing to ways to handle stress. Your peers may have some ideas or you might browse the Web for sites that address student needs. In addition to general study skills and survival tips, consider including sources related to your discipline. Regardless of what you teach, you'll find many sites that support the context of your field or provide illuminating details about topics you will cover. If your syllabus is on the Web, these links will be hot and easily accessed.

As you consider which topics to include and how you might design your syllabus or guidelines, devote some thought to word choice and layout.

Labels

While many nouns are fairly neutral, many of them carry connotations that send messages to readers. A friend once told me that when I was preparing my résumé, I should not use the word "Employment" to head the job section, because the word was too close to "Unemployment." (I switched to "Educational Positions," "Writing and Editing Positions," and so on.) With this thought in mind, I would urge you to use neutral, descriptive language to explain aspects of your course. Below, you will see some information about topics such as contact information, attendance, and grading. The two sticky topics are complaints and ground rules, both of which carry overtones of keeping everyone in line. Sometimes complaints are called "problems" or "grievances," which both sound rather ominous, too. You may want to consider "policies" or the more descriptive "protocols," which leaps over the causes and right into the process of amelioration. Similarly, "ground rules" can sound like specifications for an encounter group or camp. Many faculty and GSIs use "guidelines" or "classroom expectations."

Format and Tone

The overall design of your syllabus or class guidelines and the tone you employ will, obviously, serve as an introduction to yourself and your course. Word processing applications, with their print styles, varied sizes or types of fonts, and more, can help you create a form that looks professional, can be easily understood, and indicates to students what they should know and what they should attend.

Pay attention to headings, white space, use of bullets, and so on. We all take cues from formats. Design features guide us through a document and either draw or diminish our attention. Take advantage of these bold and subtle elements of appearance.

The tone you use in your writing also plays an important role in how you see yourself as a teacher and what you expect from students. Some GSIs feel they must convey a strong sense of authority, but the message can be clear without sounding like the gestapo. Rather, you can sound like a serious scholar and encourage colleagueship to initiate students into the academic world at its best.

Contact Information

Be thorough and specific. Let students know what to call you and when they should contact you. Note how soon they can expect to receive a response to their e-mails or phone messages. Include your department telephone number and office location, your mailbox location, and the name of your faculty supervisor or department chair and his or her number. GSIs who teach sections should add the appropriate information for the course professor.

Course Description

A course description should be a brief summary that reflects the essence of the entry in the college catalog. The description can also place the course within the larger discipline or within the requirements of a department or college and introduce course goals.

Course Goals and Learning Outcomes

Goals and outcomes provide two ways of thinking about a course. Goals provide language that focuses on the big issues of the course. Learning outcomes translate the goals into student behaviors, giving students a clear idea of what they can achieve if they do good work in the class and giving teachers a range of "products" that can be measured.

The goals of a course may seem patently obvious by the title and the department that offers it; for example, History of the United States, 1865 to Present. However, students are not going to learn about everything that has happened in that period. Goals let them know how the course is shaped, whether they can expect to learn about social unrest in the country or the extent to which policies were shaped by Supreme Court decisions, whether the focus will be centered on Washington, D.C., and the government, or if more attention will be paid to the economy, the labor movement, or the arts.

Goals are not easy to write, but new faculty and GSIs find it unexpectedly useful to go through the process of creating them. One very helpful tool is called the Teaching Goals Inventory, developed by Thomas A. Angelo and K. Patricia Cross (1993). The inventory appears in Angelo and Cross's book, *Classroom Assessment Techniques*, and on the Web as an interactive tool. Answering the 53 questions takes about 10 minutes, and the results will help you see that you may have more goals for a class (for instance, developing students' management skills or their ability to think holistically, improving their writing skills, seeing that they learn techniques to gain new knowledge in a field) than those denoted by the title and materials of the course.

The exercise of writing goals not only makes you more articulate about your course but also gives you and your students some common ground to return to from time to time. With the aid of the instructor, goals can contribute to students' understanding the big picture of the course and how it is connected to the rest of the discipline, other disciplines, and, with a little work, the rest of their education.

Here are two sample goals; the first reflects the material but lacks active accountability on the part of students; the second is broader and reflects details found in the Teaching Goal Inventory.

Tone, as you can see, plays an important role in emphasizing responsibility and involvement in a course.

> The goal of this course is to offer students opportunities to learn about the history of art in the classical world.

versus

> Students will learn to distinguish the features of Roman and Egyptian art.

Learning outcomes aim the lens at the content of the course even closer to the students and their work in the course. Outcomes are written with verbs that can be acted upon by students and measured by instructors (Module 2: Planning for Outcomes, 2006). Verbs from Bloom's Taxonomy chart on p. 19 in chapter 2 exemplify actions that function well in learning outcomes.

Here is a sample outcome that tells students about what they can expect regarding content and their responsibilities in the course:

> To successfully complete this course, you will explain through discussions, essays, and presentations the differences in Egyptian and Roman art.

The learning outcome suggests several ways instructors could assess student learning. The use of "you" rather than the impersonal "students" indicates an agency that is missing in the first two examples. Your students will process the outcome in a different way than they would the goal, because the language is direct and places responsibility for learning the material and demonstrating their knowledge squarely before them.

Calendar of Assignments and Exams

The first things students look for in a syllabus, so I've been told, are the scheduling, grading, number of exams, and information on big projects. They also look at reading assignments or problem sets to see how much work they are expected to do.

Some GSIs develop their course by themes (e.g., literature, by eras or writers or styles; history, by decades or geography or cultural aspects). Using subheadings in a syllabus can provide students with ways to consider the aspects of the whole course and also assist students in linking assignments and activities to course goals.

Be as accurate as you can in the calendar, but to avoid some of the headaches that have occurred on campuses when students treat a syllabus as a contract (which it is to a great degree) and become litigious, be sure to add a comment stating that the schedule may shift because of an alteration in the pace of the class, weather problems, or unforeseen events.

Grading Proportions and Policies

A typical grading scheme may spread points among, for example, 40% for a paper or project and 30% each for midterm and final examinations. But percentages can be reassigned for many good purposes. New faculty who have a discussion component can use points for participation. GSIs who run discussion sections or labs should ask or plead for at least 5% of the student grade. Ten is better. When points are attached to section attendance and participation, students are obviously more likely to attend and to be engaged. (Most course professors can be convinced that attendance is worth something, because of the obvious and hoped-for corollary of time-on-task to learning.)

Policies included in a syllabus may cover departmental mandates, such as a specified number of absences causing a student to fail, whether extra credit points can be earned, or the penalties for turning work in late. If you are in charge of these decisions, seek local advice about the campus customs and refer to chapter 13, "Grading." As you develop your plan, consider the consequences of each step. For instance, if you decide to be lenient about late work, how might the piling up of, say, weekly problem sets detract from student learning and the course plan? If you are completely rigid, would there be unforeseen consequences for responsible students? Unquestionably it is easier to begin with a more rigid system, though perhaps allowing one late turn-in if you have frequent assignments in your course gives students a cushion to use at their discretion and cuts down on your time needed to deal with this issue. However you design grading policies, expect them to shift with experience, with the courses you teach, and through conversations with other faculty and GSIs.

Assignment Information

The woman this book is dedicated to, Cleo Martin, taught writing in a way you might expect Gandhi to do it. To say she created a sense of serenity in a classroom is an understatement. She built an atmosphere of trust that fostered high engagement, humor, and devotion. But Cleo detested the ragged edges of sheets that had been ripped from a spiral notebook. She banned such paper from her class, and it did nothing to diminish the respect students had for her. You, too, can specify your preferences, from staples versus paper clips to a standard font versus hard-to-read script or blocky letters. Clarifying your specifications can save time and worry.

I have seen faculty and GSIs include the term's assignments *with* their syllabi. More common is the practice of describing in general terms the types of activities you will require of students and handing out assignments or putting them on the Internet at an appropriate time.

Uses of Technology

Freshmen may not have had the experience of using a course Web site. Give clear instructions and screen shots to help them as much as you can. Consider asking them to find a computer buddy or assigning a project of some sort for them to do with another student. An introductory scavenger hunt assignment is even more important if students need to learn new applications. Give them all the relevant information about computer lab locations and hours, when help is available, and other tips about your campus.

Libraries and Other Campus Resources

Include some information on campus resources, such as the library (hours, locations of depositories that students may need for your class, even location of photocopy machines if you like), labs that your course uses, and other information relevant to your class. It has become common, of course, for campus services to have Web sites, as well as brochures or fliers.

Attendance Policy

In addition to points for attendance, define policies regarding tardiness (I always tell students to come, no matter how late they might be) and departure. Many students have a tendency to begin packing up their belongings in the final five minutes of class. It is a disruptive, noisy, and rude practice. Without expressing any of the negative associations, you could make a case for the fact that you have X minutes together each week, and you want to make the most of them. Tell students that to help them get to their next class, you will always end class one minute before the official close; most students should not have a problem packing away their materials and putting their coats on in a minute.

Universitywide policies generally cover excused absences, including medical causes, participation in sports, and religious observances. The University of Iowa makes a point of noting that celebrating a win in a football game is *not* a legitimate excuse for missing class.

Syllabus tone plays a role in urging students to attend class. They, of course, want to be treated with respect and be recognized as adults. The attendance policy should promote community. I have seen syllabi where GSIs or faculty members use language such as: "You will attend every session." A student's reaction may be, "Oh yeah? Make me." If students attend class under threats, they will probably be less inclined to feel they are part of a learning community, it will feel more like a gulag, or at least high school. Defining attendance policies may be beyond your control, since colleges or departments often determine the regulations. Nevertheless, for your part, I suggest discussing the why instead of the what. Here's a sample.

Because the purpose of this section is to discuss the lecture and your homework assignments, we will be able to have richer and more rewarding sessions if everyone attends regularly. The differing viewpoints that you all
will no doubt bring to class discussions will enhance our exploration of
topics and issues.

There are any number of ways to indicate to students that (a) what goes on
in the classroom will be important, and (b) a productive learning community
depends upon the participation of all of its members.

Assistance for Students With Disabilities

Your institution should provide you with the location, Web address, and
contact numbers of the center that assists students with physical, develop-
mental, and learning disabilities. In most places, students need to contact
those programs to legitimize requests for extended test-taking time, help
with note taking, and so on. Sometimes students who had problems in high
school want to believe the problems have been left behind and will avoid
seeking help in college. Some students may not use the services available to
them until they have problems, so official notice of a student needing assistance may not arrive at the beginning of a term.

Add to your syllabus an invitation to students needing accommodations
to contact you.

Expectations for Classroom Decorum

You may think guidelines for behavior are needed only for classes that deal
with sensitive or difficult topics, but I know of a class where two young men
nearly came to fisticuffs over the proper solution to a problem in a statistics
assignment. No class seems to be entirely immune to inappropriate behavior.
The overall goal of ground rules is probably captured in the Golden Rule, a
version of which seems to be part of most cultures on the planet. (The Platinum Rule [Alessandra 1996] states that you should treat people the way they
want to be treated.)

It is completely appropriate for you to present the class with a list of
desirable expectations that might include turning off cell phones and other
electronic devices, not reading newspapers, or other expectations you have.

Depending upon your discipline and available time, one way to create a
list of guidelines is to break students into small groups on the first or second

day and ask them to list attributes of classes they have enjoyed—or problems they've witnessed. GSIs who have brought the students into this process report that when problems arise, the students themselves will mention the ground rules to those who are out of order.

Some GSIs seed discussions on ground rules with a few items from a list written by George Washington when he was sixteen. He titled it *Rules of Civility & Decent Behaviour in Company and Conversation* (Washington's School Exercises c. 1744). Here are a few of his rules; the capitalization, spelling, and punctuation are his.

- 1st Every Action done in Company, ought to be with Some Sign of Respect, to those that are Present.
- 6th Sleep not when others Speak, Sit not when others stand, Speak not when you Should hold your Peace, walk not on when others Stop.
- 61st Utter not base and frivolous things amongst grave and Learn'd Men nor very Difficult Questians or Subjects, among the Ignorant or things hard to be believed, Stuff not your Discourse with Sentences amongst your Betters nor Equals.
- 73d Think before you Speak pronounce not imperfectly nor bring out your Words too hastily but orderly & distinctly.
- 88th Be not tedious in Discourse, make not many Digressigns, nor repeat often the Same manner of Discourse.
- 110th Labour to keep alive in your Breast that Little Spark of Celestial fire Called Conscience.

Complaints—Protocols for Problems

Most universities have developed protocols for how students should go about filing complaints regarding their classmates or instructors, and your institution may have a template for you to use. Students will most likely be instructed to speak with you first, and if they are still dissatisfied, to your teaching supervisor or department chair.

Ethics

This section should include plagiarism and cheating—educational fraud—and other issues of academic dishonesty. Your institution very likely has developed detailed policies regarding these issues, and your department may prescribe templates for your syllabus or course guidelines.

You may want to add comments about fraudulently gained credentials; no one wants to drive across a bridge or have a tooth removed by an engineer or a dentist who cheated his or her way through school. Any discussion about plagiarism should begin with a clear definition of what it is and what it is not. The simplest definition is the best: Plagiarism is when you use someone's ideas without crediting them.

Tell students that it is easy to avoid plagiarizing simply by citing the sources for direct quotations or an author's ideas. I think it is worth adding in your remarks that you have heard that in some high school classes students could copy material from the Web without citing the source. Some faculty and GSIs include in their syllabus examples of proper and improper methods of citation for books, journals, interviews, and Web sites. If students will be writing papers needing this information, you do them and yourself a favor by putting it at their fingertips.

You may find it helpful to review chapter 12, "Fraud, Cheating, Plagiarism, and Some Assignments That Discourage It," before you decide what to put into your syllabus. Be prepared for the fact that some students are oblivious to what constitutes plagiarism and some are terrified of doing it unintentionally.

If your course involves using human subjects in some capacity, discuss those policies and practices here, too.

The syllabus provides a foundation of expectations for your students. It explains some of the institutional expectations and describes your standards. While it outlines the rules of the class, it also gives students a strong sense of who you are as a teacher and a human being. A clear, thorough, and warm syllabus will help set a tone that will serve all of you well throughout the term.

References

Alessandra, T. (1996). *The platinum rule: Relationship strategies for connecting with anyone.* Retrieved August 20, 2006, from http://www.alessandra.com/about_platinumrule/index.asp

Angelo, T. A., & Cross, K. P. (1993). *Classroom assessment techniques: A handbook for college teachers.* San Francisco: Jossey-Bass.

Duffy, D. K., & Jones, J. W. (1995). *Teaching within the rhythms of the semester.* San Francisco: Jossey-Bass.

Grunert, J. (1997) *The course syllabus: A learning-centered approach.* Boston: Anker Publications.

Module 2: Planning for outcomes (2006). *Developing learning outcomes.* Retrieved January 30, 2007, from http://www.league.org/gettingresults/web/module2/learning/index.html

Washington's School Exercises: Rules of Civility and Decent Behaviour in Company and Conversation. (c. 1744). *The Papers of George Washington.* Retrieved December 4, 2007, from http://gwpapers.virginia.edu/documents/civility/transcript.html

5

PAUSING TO ASSESS
AND REFRESH

While education and testing go hand in hand, assessing students before course work begins often slips through the cracks. Time is so short, but a great deal of good can be gained by **Finding Out What Your Students Know**—(learning about their misconceptions)—**and Helping Them Change Their Minds**. In addition to using pre- and postassessments for individual students, using any number of **Classroom Assessments** can help instructors keep a finger on the pulse of class perceptions, which of course influence performance.

Finding Out What Your Students Know—and Helping Them Change Their Minds

A friend recalls seeing a public service film when he was in grade school in the 1950s. The movie included a scene with a sad and dejected man sitting on a park bench and wearing a suit and fedora. The man was described as being divorced. My friend's father did not wear a fedora, or any kind of hat, and neither did the fathers of his friends. So, my friend, in his youth, analyzed the information and drew the conclusion that men who wore hats were divorced. Eventually, of course, he learned that he was mistaken.

Such constructions of knowledge are not limited to children. Consider interpretations of scientific and historic events that have been considered "the final word" for decades or centuries, and then further experiments are made, or a mind with a different viewpoint examines and reinterprets the evidence in such a way to completely revise the commonly held belief. Examples are rife, from the round earth to the heliocentric solar system to more recent scientific revolutions such as the geology of tectonic plates and the possibility of infant heart surgery. Recently the role of lactic acid and muscle pain has finally been accepted as a false scientific truth (Kolata, 2006). It took the man who questioned the conventionally held beliefs more than thirty years of research to prove his proposition, during which time his peer group rejected his claims, his articles, and his arguments.

Current scientific knowledge creates our reality, so established facts in our time seem obvious, but all such findings were, at one time, completely dismissed by the best practitioners in the field as outrageous and perhaps even blasphemous.

Educators need to be aware that students, like my friend with the fedora-equals-divorce theory, may hold ideas from previous experiences that are wrong. The human urge to evaluate and analyze available data gives students (like all of us) confidence in their knowledge—at least until it is challenged. Once they (or we) have made sense of a certain section of information, our tendency is to hold on to the paradigms we have created and be both less aware and perhaps even dismissive of new and possibly relevant information that conflicts with what we believe. Another recent indicator of this phenomenon was sadly revealed in news stories reporting research findings of the dispiriting revelation that one-fifth—*one-fifth*—of Americans believe the sun orbits the earth (Ventura, 2005). How can this ignorance persist, we wonder? But these sorts of misconceptions, along with confusion about geography, basic physics, and history, do prevail, year after year, survey after survey.

A documentary titled *A Private Universe* (Schneps & Sadler, 1987) filmed at Harvard University and a nearby middle school, illustrates this very phenomenon of clinging to early adopted beliefs. Responding to questions about the cause of the seasonal changes and the phases of the moon, the graduating seniors at Harvard are extremely confident and articulate as they explain their faulty beliefs. Some of them hold the same ideas as the more hesitant 13-year-olds at a Boston middle school.

Students will obviously enter your classroom with some set beliefs, and they will not understand that they hold biases or false notions because the beliefs are simply "their universe." They will be reluctant to accept the possibility that they may have been mis- or undereducated, or that new research has revealed such startling findings that their beliefs need to be dismantled and rebuilt. Your task is to create methods for discovering and revealing students' misapprehensions. Asking students to explain *why* can be the most effective method for uncovering false ideas, and these explanations can be part of written or oral activities. Then students must be encouraged to change their ideas.

One of the most important occurrences in college is for students to change their minds—expanding or modifying their thinking in any number of ways. Typically, people think college is for learning information, and it is. But it is not only about adding discrete facts; it is about unlearning and relearning, and it is about forging new paths and connections that create fresh understandings and expand the way minds work. Students need to be told and reminded that they should expect their mindscape to be redesigned in college, with portions of knowledge being questioned and dismantled for good cause, with the results that new associations will create revised constructions. This very process is one of the most important activities of college. Thus, one of the most important examples faculty members and GSIs can provide to students through explication and the simple act of pondering is that educated people are open to new information, though they then question it, examine it, and evaluate it—sometimes for many years—to see if it revises or supports previously held opinions or beliefs, or whether it deserves to lead to a change of mind. Examples of new and good information being ignored or at least held at bay for decades or generations are part of most disciplines.

Fred Antczak, professor of English at Grand Valley State University, Allendale, Michigan, tells the story of a classroom experience when he was a student at the University of Chicago (F. Antczak, personal communication, March 10, 1998). His professor, Wayne Booth, a prominent literary critic at the University of Chicago who always taught a course to undergraduates, paused one day to evaluate the class's discussion. He announced that a new insight raised by students' comments was making him change the way he thought about a particular concept. After the session, a student approached him and told him that her parents were not paying the university's high tuition so that her professor could change his mind. He answered that such an event was in fact precisely why they were spending their good money.

Share stories with your students about developments in your field that altered set ideas. Invite them to tell their own stories about things they once thought but after acquiring new information decided to change their minds. Remind students that children and academics alike hold private universes, and that sometimes the universes need to be shaken and revised. Putting an issue like this on the table will create an atmosphere where students will more likely admit their faulty thinking and open themselves to the often hard work of revising their ideas.

One effective method of helping students clarify their knowledge was developed by Eric Mazur, physics professor at Harvard University who founded Project Galileo in 1990 to explore educational innovations such as Peer Instruction and Just-in-Time-Teaching. Mazur wanted to use student interaction to improve learning. "The problem with education . . . is not the method of presentation—it is the assimilation of material presented" (Mazur, 2006).

The Mazur Group developed ways to poll students in large groups to assess their understanding of foundational concepts. For example, Mazur interrupts his lecture every 15 to 20 minutes to present a question on the screen that probes basic understanding of a concept under discussion. The question, which may include an illustration, offers four answers. Students have a handheld device—called a clicker—that they can use to submit an answer and also send another signal to gauge their level of confidence in the answer.

Once students submit their first responses, they talk among themselves for a minute, which Mazur times. Then Mazur offers them a chance to submit a second answer and a second level of confidence. Finally, he confirms the right answer. This method of immediate testing of one's knowledge and gaining feedback on the correct answers obviously helps students set their notions straight.

You can adapt this to your own class and discipline using the ever more common clickers. Of course a show of hands or pencil on paper can be used as well.

Classroom Assessments

As class gets under way and nerves are diminishing, names are becoming familiar, and the community has started to coalesce, you may want to use a number of assessment tools to help establish baselines of knowledge or to check on the progress of your students in ways that are unrelated to exams, quizzes, or assignments.

Classroom assessments help you learn about your students' perceptions of the class, what is going well for them, and about problems they're having or what they would like to change. In addition to the methods described below, you can find scores of techniques detailed in *Classroom Assessment Techniques: A Handbook for College Teachers* (Angelo & Cross, 1993).

One-Minute Paper

One brief method that is widely used is called a one-minute paper. Hand out file cards or ask students to take out half a sheet of paper. Ask one question, give students a minute or so to write about it, and collect the results.

Questions to ask include:

- How is the pace of this class working for you?
- What has most helped (or hindered) your learning in this class?
- Is there some learning activity you would like to be doing in this class that we either don't do or we don't do often enough?
- What was the most important thing you learned today?
- What are you confused about from today's class?

And so on. You can ask about course materials or activities or how well students can understand you, or anything else that is germane to your course or would improve the progress of the term.

Since responses are anonymous, they need no grading or comments. Review them after class and at the following class give a brief summary in an aggregate form. Outlying responses should be noted in some fashion, too, so that all voices are honored. Sometimes "outliers" give off-the-cuff answers, such as, "This is dumb." Give them a nod by saying, "A few students thought the exercise was a waste of time. I'm sorry about that. Others had some suggestions/opinions/confusions that I'd like to address."

A point Angelo and Cross (1993) make is not to ask questions you don't want the answers to. For instance, if you sense some large problems and ask a question that uncorks a lot of frustrations, you may feel too overwhelmed by the responses to create a remedy. Preventing such situations is, of course, the ideal. The timely and early use of a one-minute paper can be a helpful method for detecting any nascent problems.

Midterm Evaluations

Some GSIs decide to create a list (paper or courseware) of questions for students to answer anonymously at midterm. The great benefit of this activity is that unlike end-of-term evaluations, where instructors no longer have an opportunity to alter anything, midterm responses may offer some ideas for immediate changes. If you decide to perform such an evaluation, tell students about this benefit to rationalize the time it will take. Once you've received the responses, collate them and bring a brief summary back to the students. If you plan to implement changes, discuss them, and if there are things you cannot change (textbook, exam schedule, and so on), offer some sympathy, tell them you'd be happy to talk about these issues outside class, and move on.

Here are some questions to include in such an evaluation. The sample formats include open-ended examples, forced-selection examples, and checklists. Consider the kinds of information you want to receive and then mix and match formats to create the most effective form (Figure 5.1).

A Class Evaluation by an Outsider

On many campuses, the faculty development office provides another type of evaluation. The format of this method, which is often called a Small Group Instructional Diagnosis (SGID),[1] calls for a neutral party to come into the class, gather students into small groups, and ask each group to answer these questions:

> What is your teacher doing that improves your learning?
> What does your teacher do that inhibits your learning?
> What suggestions do you have for your teacher?

Some faculty developers add a fourth question:

> What could you yourself do to improve your learning?

This final prompt reminds students that they, too, have responsibilities to fulfill. Following the process of gathering the responses, which is designed to take about 20 minutes, the person who came to your room will collate the responses and meet with you to discuss the student comments. One great benefit of this method is that the anonymity goes a long way to ensure authentic responses of praise and criticism. If your campus doesn't offer the service, you might ask a peer to do it for you.

---

[1] The process was developed by Donald Wulff (1985), Center for Instructional Development and Research, University of Washington, Seattle, Washington. The method was first described by Clark and Bekey (1979).

FIGURE 5.1
Sample Questions for Midterm Evaluations

1. Are there parts of the material that you would like more help learning? Please be specific in your answer.

2. Are there activities that either contribute to or distract from your learning? Please explain.

3. If you could change one thing about the course, what would it be?

4. To what extent is the course fulfilling your expectations?

Not much	*Sufficient*	*Exceeding*
1	3	5

5. Which of the following activities have most aided your learning? (Please check the most effective activity.)
   _____ Paired conferences
   _____ Spontaneous debates
   _____ Group quizzes
   _____ My notes on your lab work
   _____ Instant grading of lab work

6. Would you prefer that we rely more or less on Web resources?
   _____ More
   _____ Less
   _____ Not sure

Some instructors, depending upon the rapport they have with their class, add a question such as:
   How do you like college so far?
   Do you like living in _____?

In my experience, faculty members and GSIs were rarely surprised by the results, though occasionally students made an unexpected suggestion. In one case, they asked that the overhead projector be raised slightly; why students had not make the request during class is baffling, but they hadn't.

Sometimes students express concerns about understanding their instructor's accent or the amount of reading or the types of assignments. The good thing about hearing these comments is that you can talk with students about their thoughts and either work to improve something or provide a rationale that will explain why things are the way they are. In any event, tackling some issues during the semester and showing students that you want to improve the classroom is the sort of thing that can have a positive impact on the way the class works and on your effectiveness as a teacher.

Pre- and Postknowledge Assessment

Beginning the course with a content knowledge assessment can serve students and instructors in several ways. You and the students can gauge what students do and do not know so you can adjust the course in some ways.

Prepare this assessment by reflecting on the goals you've written and on the course content. Consider people, events, theories, locations, jargon, phenomena, equations, or other items you hope will become part of what they know well by the time they leave the class. Select 10 or 12 topics and list them on the left side of a sheet of paper. Across the top, write 1–4 and instruct students to check the number (1 for "know nothing about this," 2 for "somewhat familiar," 3 for "know something about it," or 4 for "feel fairly knowledgeable") for each item. It is important to emphasize that while this sheet may look like a test, it is not. It assesses their confidence in some knowledge rather than the knowledge itself.

You should think about whether to ask students to submit the information anonymously. This version may elicit more honest responses, since none of us like to admit we don't know things. On the other hand, if students do include their names, you will have information to measure their progress. A benefit to them is that you can return the papers and they will have them as a reference for their studies during the term.

One way to use this information is that if you discover that all but a few students are informed about a topic, you might excuse everyone else a few minutes early one day and provide some intense tutoring or give students advice on Web help or other self-education strategies.

The major benefit of this exercise is that instructors learn what students already know about the field or at least whether students are familiar with some of the terms. Teachers at all levels can be more focused and responsive in their teaching when they have this information. You might even modify classroom activities on the spot, such as:

- When a given subject arises, you might say, "I know five of you feel well informed here, so when you break into small groups, would you identify yourselves, so one of you can go to each group?"

- Or, you may put the five in their own group so that they can discuss something at the next level.

Partway through the term, or at the end, hand out the same sheet, and invite students once again to mark the appropriate places for their sense of competence regarding knowledge of these topics. A comparison of this aggregate assessment of your class reveals the students' advancing knowledge— something that is gratifying to them as well as to you.

One new instructor who used this assessment told me that at the beginning of the term, students had marked high confidence on some topics they felt well informed about. As the course unfolded and their learning expanded, they realized how much they had not known initially. Their marks on the sheet slid from high confidence to middling confidence, but for good reason, since their knowledge had grown substantially as had their understanding that there was a great deal more to know.

What I Know, What I'd Like to Know (WIK, WILK)

An idea that you might use for a course or for a topic within a course is the WIK, WILK. Pass out file cards and ask students to write WIK on one side and WILK on the other and complete each side of the card. You might briefly demonstrate this exercise by picking a topic you're interested in—for example, curling, Mozambique, monoprints—and listing what you know and what you'd like to know. The example will provide a model of brainstorming and also show students that you're not afraid to admit to not knowing some things. The information you gather from students can help you structure your teaching and help you decide what to emphasize or deemphasize. These cards can also be filled in by pairs or groups in conversation—What Some of Us Know, What Some of Us Would Like to Know. When students gather and confess to a few other students about the gaps in their knowledge, their esprit de corps is enhanced and they are likely to feel more comfortable asking questions. Results could go on the course Web site for future reference and discussion.

Middles

Middles require refreshment—physical and mental. If a class session drags along with a tone that feels more like fatigue than excitement, remember the accepted notion of the 20-minute attention span, and ask students to stand up midway. This loss of concentration can sometimes be countered by other interruptions—laughter, talking, eating, writing, physical movement, a video clip.

A break will generally be unnecessary if you use a variety of active learning techniques, since they give students the opportunity to move around, talk with one another, laugh, engage in a writing or board activity, or in some other way refresh themselves. Students in labs and studios, of course, are generally active, both physically and in conversation, though instructors often schedule a break because of the length of the class.

The middles of terms can also do with some reenergizing. Plan some unique activities for midterm to help your students recharge their batteries. Changes in routine will be welcomed by most students—as they are for most of us. Some ideas:

- field trip (even a very brief one on campus)
- guest speaker
- different media from what they're accustomed to
- debate*
- fishbowl discussion*
- mini-presentations*
- fresh active learning strategy

  * Variations are described in detail in chapter 8 on running discussions.

If you plan a field trip or invite a speaker, be sure to do the required preparation so that the activity is an effective learning opportunity. Field trips off campus may require university or departmental permission. Be sure to plan for students who may need special accommodations. With guests, be specific about your expectations. Prepare students so they understand what they can gain from the speaker. Explore ways the visit will connect to course goals. Plan methods for students to engage with the guest through their preparation of questions. Don't hesitate to ask a speaker to use only a portion of the class. Follow presentations immediately or at the next session with opportunities for students to evaluate information or otherwise process what they've seen or heard.

Endings

Courses typically end with a final examination or project, and that's that. Adios. Most institutions also require that students evaluate the course and the teacher.

Enrich the ending of a course with some other activities. Below are a few ideas.

- Give students the postknowledge survey described previously. This exercise supplies a bookend that lets students see for themselves how their knowledge has grown during the term.
- Invite students to write a letter to students who take the course in the future. This option also invites students to reflect on the course, its content, the studying demanded, the text, and other resources. Students can do this exercise anonymously, of course, and to allow them more privacy, you can bring a large envelope that can be sealed, and then make arrangements to receive the packet after you have finished your grading responsibilities. Segments of these letters used at the beginning of future classes can supply powerful testimonials.
- Connect the dots. Engage your students in an exercise where you all pursue the goal of providing the context for the course by describing the big picture of the course, how it fits into the discipline, or even how it fits into a larger scope of knowledge. Since many students do not generally see the wholeness of their education, it is useful to push them into some reflection by preparing several statements that begin: "In this course, you have (studied, researched, solved, written, or discussed) . . . Put them into small groups to brainstorm about their accomplishments. Remind them of how these items may well connect with their lives 5, 10, or 20 years in the future. Use phrases such as, "You have taken responsibility" and "You have used your initiative." This language reminds them that they have exercised control of their learning. It can set an example for their future.
- Give them a class assessment sheet. Some prompts might be:
  - When I signed up for this course, I expected:
  - The most challenging part of the course for me was:
  - The most important knowledge I gained was:
  - If I could change one thing about the class, it would be:

Students are accustomed to no closure beyond exams. Some of the suggestions above may offer students quite a different way of thinking about the course after it's over.

Classroom assessments administered by instructors are still a fairly new undertaking in colleges and universities. In addition to the types of assessment described here, Angelo and Cross (1993), as noted earlier, describe hundreds in their book, giving information about how long it takes to administer the assessments and how much time it takes instructors to review the results.

With the growth of student-centered learning and the expectations that go along with classes operating as communities of learners, it seems natural and sensible to conduct ongoing assessments as part of the educational whole.

References

Angelo, T. A., & Cross, K. P. (1993). *Classroom assessment techniques: A handbook for college teachers*. San Francisco: Jossey-Bass.

Clark, D. J., & Bekey, J. (1979). Use of small groups in instructional evaluation. *Journal of the Professional and Organizational Development Network in Higher Education, 1,* 87–95.

Kolata, G. (2006, May 17). Lactic acid is not muscles' foe, it's fuel. *The New York Times.* Retrieved May 17, 2006, from http://www.nytimes.com/2006/05/16/health/nutrition/16run.html?ex = 130543   2000&en = 2778e99d7eab85a6&ei = 5090&partner = rssuserland&emc = rss

Mazur, E. (2006). No magic bullet. *Mazur Group.* Retrieved January 8, 2007, from http://mazur-www.harvard.edu/research/detailspage.php?ed = 1&rowid = 52

Schneps, M. H., & Sadler, P. M. (Writers/Directors). (1987). *A private universe* [Videotape]. (Available from Harvard-Smithsonian Center for Astrophysics, Science Education Department, Science Media Group. Washington, DC: Annenberg/CPB: Pyramid Film and Video)

Ventura, Michael. (2005, January 21). Letters at 3AM. *Austin Chronicle.* Retrieved August 1, 2006, from http://www.austinchronicle.com/gyrobase/Issue/column?oid = oid%3A255074

Wulff, D. H., Staton-Spicer, A. Q., Hess, C. W., & Nyquist, J. D. (1985). The student perspective on evaluating teaching effectiveness. *ACA Bulletin, 53,* 39–47.

6

STUDENTS—WHAT THEY EXPECT AND WHAT YOU MIGHT EXPECT

This book is about embracing teaching and students. This chapter addresses some of the expectations on both sides. Diversity has been a code word for racial minorities, but realistically you can expect many more personal attributes among your **Student Constituents,** including gender, race, ethnicity, religion, class, age, students with disabilities, athletes, and celebrities.

Although some people still deny the phenomenon of **Grade Inflation**, evidence of it has been with us for well over a decade. Another consideration that has arisen in the last generation is the **Notion of Students as Customers**.

New college students wonder about many things when they walk into your classroom, but they may be reluctant to raise their hands, meaning that **Your Students' Unasked Questions** might remain unasked. Beyond the questions students may withhold are ones they may not know they're harboring, including whether there are ways to help them improve their learning. You may find ideas in **Preparing Your Students for Learning—Mnemonics and Beyond**. A specific tool that is used by some instructors is **Mandatory Conferences**. Others pursue information regarding **Learning Styles** in an effort to enhance student learning.

Most students arrive at college with hopes and assumptions about roommates, about campus life and culture, and about classes. Preconceptions seeded by media, friends, or relatives, campus visits and promotional material all lay the groundwork for the assumptions new students carry with them about their own academic performance and the behaviors of teachers and other students.

For those students who are beyond their first year or returning after a hiatus, assumptions will still abound, but they will now be heavily influenced by their previous campus experiences and those of their peers.

If you are a GSI, new students especially will probably have one of three overarching expectations about you. They will assume you are a professor, or they will have heard about GSIs and feel cheated because they don't have a full professor, or they will know about GSIs from varied sources and accept you. It is often the case that rumors and confusion abound regarding GSIs. Try to ignore them. You have a class to teach, and there is no pressing need to explore the ranks of instructors. Many students may, in fact, welcome the idea of having a GSI because GSIs are often nearer to their age, and you may seem less intimidating than an older and perhaps more reserved professor. If students have heard upperclassmen or older siblings rave about their great GSIs, the students will be happy to see you.

If you are a new faculty member and bear the title assistant professor, most students will not distinguish that title or the implied level of experience from any other. They will, of course, notice if you are young, as the media often relies on mature and often white male academics to supply the professorial character in a movie or television program.

Students expect particular behaviors from instructors, including an authoritative voice and manner and vast knowledge. They are right to expect these things. New faculty know a great deal more than students do about content and learning in all its forms. This is true even for the GSI who is merely four or five years older than the classroom of students. Reflecting on your own studies and accomplishments can help project the authority students expect.

Student Constituents—Gender, Race, Ethnicity, Religion, Class, Age, Students With Disabilities, Athletes, and Celebrities

Resources abound on student constituencies. Caring about and showing respect to individuals is the common starting point, as is the Golden Rule.

Instructors can improve the dynamics of their classes by considering their own assumptions, setting an appropriate example, or leading a class discussion on assumptions. Differences among class members create part of the wealth of a college education. A good assumption to carry into the classroom is to believe that all students expect to learn a great deal and participate in a meaningful way. New teachers, whether faculty members or GSIs, may have apprehensions about interacting with and teaching students who belong to groups they have never had contact with, such as older students or a student with cerebral palsy or a Muslim woman in a head scarf or students whose dress or posture seems to indicate zero interest in learning. Indeed, the instructors may belong to a minority group and wonder about how they are being perceived. The best place to begin is by focusing on the substance of the course and to use that commonality as the rallying point again and again as all members of the class learn to work together and to understand one another.

Below are a few pitfalls and considerations.

Individuals Representing Their Groups

Not too many years ago, some GSIs and faculty members who had one or two members of a minority in their class would expect that person to give voice to the group they came from. How humiliating to be singled out. Could you imagine speaking on behalf of men or women or Irish Americans or Cubans or Californians? No single individual can speak for a group. Wherever we come from and whichever attributes we carry give us experience, and your students may wish to use their backgrounds when they speak on various topics in class, but let them make the choice, and reinforce the idea that their experience is simply that—*their experience*; another person from a similar background may have drawn quite different conclusions. Talk about this assumption and prevent students from being singled out to respond to a particular question because of what they look or sound like.

Students With Disabilities

Students, regardless of abilities or disabilities, are students first. People with disabilities have worked hard to wipe out the labels that have been attached to them for decades. Instructors can further promote their cause by simply treating them as students. This does not preclude approaching people in wheelchairs, for instance, and offering to help them find a suitable location in the classroom.

Some students will arrive with learning disabilities, but you will not know it. They may approach you after class, especially if you note the section in your syllabus regarding the fact that you will make accommodations to those who contact you. The students need to register with the office that oversees students with disabilities in order to obtain accommodations, which might include assistance with note taking, isolation during exams, books on tape, extended periods for exams, and so on. Instructors can expect to work with the designated offices in helping these students reach their educational goals.

In the classroom, assume that all students are there to focus on the course work, to work together, and to learn.

Athletes and Other Celebrities

In large universities in particular, many athletes are drafted into colleges for their physical skills. Many of them are top-notch students, but many, too, need extra help, such as required study times, tutoring, and so on. It can be intimidating for an instructor to receive their roll lists and discover a name they've seen in the newspaper headlines.

David Perlmutter (2003), associate professor of mass communication at Louisiana State University at Baton Rouge, wrote an essay that appeared in *The Chronicle of Higher Education* in which he recounted his realization that student athletes felt they were overlooked—literally, as an assumed favor—in class and that they were not expected to do particularly well. It is important to realize that athletes are students first, and they expect to be treated as students. Many of them would prefer not to have their role in sports pointed out at all by teachers.

It may be that you have celebrities of other kinds in your class—children of the rich and famous, students who have made a public mark on their own in some way, or even the dean's daughter. These students, too, should be presumed to have left their public accomplishments and connections at the door and should be assumed to be members of your learning community.

Grade Inflation

Although a few researchers deny that grade inflation has occurred in the past decades (Wonacott, 2003), data from various sources contradict those opinions. The College Board reports that the average GPA of seniors heading to college in 1994 was 3.15; in 2004, the number was 3.28 (Lewin, 2005). A similar rise is reflected in figures from the Institute of Education Sciences (n.d.), which found that the average GPAs of all high school graduates in 1990 was 2.68; in 2000, the number was 2.94.

From the news stories appearing around the country, the story of Garfield High School in Seattle, Washington, is not unique. In 2005, Garfield had 44 valedictorians—about a tenth of the entire senior class (Thompson, 2005). The causes are probably numerous, but one factor that must be included in the mix is the voice of parents. Thomas Guskey, professor of education at the University of Kentucky, says that the hairsplitting over GPAs in schools that use decimal points to the third place (the hundredths) has sent parents to court.

Grade inflation in high schools of course affects college students. A professor I knew who taught at Johns Hopkins University in Baltimore in the mid-1990s told me that a student's father telephoned him to complain and solicit for a higher grade after the professor gave the man's son a B plus.

The reasons for grade inflation are complex, and the competition for some graduate or professional programs and varied scholarships and fellowships no doubt contributes to students' desire to stay at the top, but faculty and GSIs need to be aware that the trend will mean your students' expectations may sometimes create some challenging situations. Chapter 13 offers information and suggestions about grading, some of which may help you forestall problems. Once upon a time, new college freshmen were told to expect *C*s, that *B*s were difficult to earn, and *A*s were rare. I have not heard of students receiving this pronouncement for a long time.

The Notion of Students as Customers

Since the early 1990s, some portion of students, their parents, and some administrators and faculty have been buying into the notion that students are or ought to be thought of as consumers who are owed the product they purchased with their tuition dollars (Snare, 1997). In a 2001 symposium at Harvard University on 21st-century challenges to undergraduate education, the consumerism model of higher education received a lot of attention. Susan G. Pederson, professor of history and dean of undergraduate education at Harvard said that she believed that if consumerism drives parents to call her, it is a good thing. "They keep us honest," she said. She also uses the calls as an opportunity to remind parents that a college education is not equivalent to purchasing a service. Rather, she reminds them that their sons and daughters "have entered a partnership of learning. . . . You can't bestow learning on someone. They have to want it," she said (Potier, 2001, paragraph 6). If students or parents raise this discussion with you, quote Pederson. Students are not widgets. Credit hours are not purchased like pounds of butter. The business of higher education is intellectual work, which is an activity that is almost as far as one can imagine from industrialized mass production.

Your Students' Unasked Questions

Your class will prosper in many ways if you are explicit about several things that are often ignored or simply left unattended. Some years ago I wrote a paper titled *Ten Unspoken Questions From New College Students During the First Days of Class* (Lieberg, 1998). Here are the questions.

1. What should I call you?
2. Why is the syllabus *soooo* long?
3. I wonder how you expect papers to be written.
4. How tough are exams? What if I get sick and have to leave in the middle?
5. Wow, never heard that accent. What if I can't understand you well enough?
6. Will I have to say anything out loud in this class?
7. I added up pages in my course books and came up with over 3,000! Do I have to read them all?
8. The class is so large. Does anybody really care if I come late or leave early?
9. How will I know what's important in this class?
10. What if I have a question? Office hours are a nice idea, but you look sort of scary.

Some version of these questions may have crossed your own mind when you entered college. By exercising a degree of empathy with that "new student" predicament, instructors can bridge the gap between the novice college student and the experienced academic by offering information about unasked questions—these or others.

Preparing Your Students for Learning—Mnemonics and Beyond

Your students have been learning for years, but instructors can help students improve their learning by describing a few methods to help manage the knowledge they gain. Because we now live in the cyberworld, using the idea of hypertext as a metaphor may resonate with students. Reading one section leads to references on other topics and on and on. Courses and their components should not be in a labeled box stuck on a mental shelf. Rather, content and process should be linked to what students have learned previously, to things they want to learn, to other courses, and to the broader culture. This linking will support two things: remembering and making meaning.

Didn't we all learn mnemonic tools as children, such as Every Good Boy Does Fine for the notes on the lines of a musical staff? Some tools are nonsense, but they work well enough to provide a foundation to build more knowledge. Some of your students may have read Will Cleveland and Mark Alvarez's (1997) *Yo, Millard Fillmore: And All Those Other Presidents You Don't Know* to learn the names of the U.S. presidents in proper order. The book uses a story line with key words that link to the names.

The point of list learning is that it provides a chain of words that can be used to create links with relevant knowledge. As students learn about compelling aspects of U.S. history, for example—immigration and settlement, growth of transportation, exports and imports, the rise and fall of economic development, civil rights for one group or another, media, wars, public and private education, health care, and so on—their understandings will be that much richer if they can recall congruent or linked events. Adding global events, personalities, natural disasters, and inventions contributes even more to their gaining a broad view of the world.

Mandatory Conferences

Some faculty and GSIs require every student to come to office hours during an early part of the semester—the second and third week, for instance. The focus of these conferences is often to get acquainted rather than to deal with assignments, though the structure of some classes would lend themselves to the meeting's having a dual function.

One result of these early sessions, so I have been told repeatedly, is that it helps the students become much more comfortable in class much sooner. Thus, the learning community develops more quickly, and students are apparently more likely to participate at a higher level earlier in the term.

Learning Styles

Howard Gardner (1993) opened the door to considering ways that people learn outside conventionally accepted methods, when he published *Frames of Mind: Theory of Multiple Intelligences*. His work has spawned further exploration of learning styles, some of which led to the development of self-surveys.

One survey that I have recommended is the brief, learner-oriented VARK Questionnaire (Fleming, 2006). The letters in the acronym stand for visual, aural, reading and writing, and kinesthetic. Developed by Chuck Bonwell, a historian with interest in active learning, and Neil Fleming, a secondary school and college educator from New Zealand, the survey consists of sixteen questions. The authors make it clear in their introduction to the survey that the findings are not at all related to anyone's biological wiring but rather to habits people have developed as favored methods to receive information.

Based on responses to questions such as the preferred way to be directed to a location—by landmarks or with a map, VARK offers study suggestions to students, including creating a flow chart, reading notes aloud, and so on. Suggestions are also offered on how to study most effectively when preparing for exams.

Another tool is *The Index of Learning Styles*, which was designed by chemical engineers Richard Felder and Barbara Solomon (n.d.). Their instrument contains 44 questions and results in descriptions that fall along the axes of active and reflective, sensing and intuitive, visual and verbal, sequential and global.

Unsurprisingly, the interest in learning styles led to a curiosity about teaching styles. The late Tony Grasha investigated that phenomenon and conducted workshops to help faculty determine their teaching style and to decide how best to use it to facilitate student learning. Grasha's and Laurie Richlin's book, *Teaching With Style* (1996), describes attributes of teachers, provides a self-take survey, and offers suggestions on how to use a teaching style to the best advantage.

If self-surveys help people reflect on and analyze their behaviors or lead them to a greater understanding of how they learn or teach, or to ways they could shape information they are trying to learn or present, the exercise is of value.

Whether you are a faculty member or a GSI, you may wonder if it is appropriate to include a paragraph about surveys in your syllabus or whether it is a good use of time to administer them to students during class, or you may wonder if others on campus are the ones to deal with self-assessments. These are good questions to ask. You have to decide for yourself.

I do think that encouraging people to be more reflective about their learning is an appropriate function for teachers. If students gain this sort of knowledge about themselves, they may decide to learn and practice skills that will serve them well in college and beyond.

References

Cleveland, W., & Alvarez, M. Illustrations by Nation, T. (1997). *Yo, Millard Fillmore! and all those other presidents you don't know.* Brookfield, CT: Millbrook Press.

Felder, R., & Solomon, B. (n.d.). *The index of learning styles.* Retrieved August 15, 2006, from http://www.ncsu.edu/felder-public/ILSpage.html

Fleming, N. (2006) VARK questionnaire: How do I learn best? *VARK: A guide to learning styles.* Retrieved July 20, 2006, from http://www.vark-learn.com/english/page.asp?p = questionnaire

Gardner, H. (1993). *Frames of mind: The theory of multiple intelligences.* New York: Basic Books.

Grasha, A., & Richlin, L. (1996). *Teaching with style: A practical guide to enhancing learning by understanding teaching and learning styles.* Noida, India: Alliance Publishers. Available in pdf format from http://homepages.ius.edu/kwigley/teaching_with_style.pdf

Institute of Education Sciences. National Center for Education Statistics. (n.d.). *The high school transcript study.* Retrieved August 1, 2006, from http://nces.ed.gov/ssbr/pages/transcript.asp?IndID = 15

Lewin, T. (August 17, 2005). Many going to college are not ready, report says. *The New York Times.* Retrieved August 17, 2005, from http://www.nytimes.com/glogin?URI = http://www.nytimes.com/2005/08/17/educ atio n/17scores.html& OQ = _rQ3D1&OP = 258a6ba3Q2FhQ5E5Vh2@UJx@@oQ27hQ2711Q5Ch1Q 24hN.h52eUQ3Fo)@Q3DhN.JU@x5JQ6ogoKO

Lieberg, C. (1998). *Ten unspoken questions from new college students during the first days of class*. Retrieved February 8, 2006, from http://www.uiowa.edu/%7Ecen teach/resources/ideas/greatbegin.html

Perlmutter, D. D. (2003, October 10). Black athletes and white professors: A twilight zone of uncertainty. *The Chronicle of Higher Education, 50*(07), B7.

Potier, B. (2001, October 18). Teaching or research? Students or consumers? *Harvard University Gazette*. Retrieved May 15, 2006, from http://www.hno.harvard.edu/gazette/2001/10.18/11-education.html

Snare, C. E. (1997, September). Commentary: Implications of considering students as consumers. *College Teaching, 45*(4), 122. Retrieved May 10, 2006, from http://findarticles.com/p/articles/mi_hb056/is_199709/ai_hibm1G120189221

Thompson, L. (2005, June 15). One high school—44 valedictorians. *Seattle Times*. Retrieved August 1, 2006, from http://seattletimes.nwsource.com/html/local news/2002336475_garfield15m.html

Wonacott, M. E. (2003). *Everyone goes to college: Myths and realities 25*. Retrieved July 8, 2006, from http://www.cete.org/acve/textonly/docgen.asp?tbl = mr&ID = 115

7

PREPARATION FOR
DISCUSSIONS

When you think about class discussions, do you ever imagine that you could expect virtually **One Hundred Percent Participation** from students? Has it occurred to you that class discussions might profit by **Creating Guidelines *With* Students**? Another key aspect of a good discussion is **A Safe Environment**, which includes creating an atmosphere where students can ask the "dumb question" as well as express disagreement. You will also want to establish the importance of **Learning Names—Everyone's Task**. Instructors benefit from preparing strategies to use once they observe **Who Speaks and Who Doesn't**, as well as **Who Talks Too Much**. Finally, depending upon the course, you may be concerned about **Dealing With Difficult Topics: Taboos, Personal Values, and Hurt or Angry Feelings** or wondering whether to include **Humor**. Once you have considered these classroom issues, you can turn to the task of **Preparing Content**. Defining and using **Session Goals** provides a useful guide through the class. Another common tool for conducting class, one that has become ubiquitous, is **PowerPoint**, which can add immensely to the visuals of a class, but it has some disadvantages, too, that are worth pondering.

One Hundred Percent Participation

Despite the obvious nature of discussion sections or lecture-discussion courses, many students expect to be as quiet in these classes as they are in those that are designated as strictly lectures. When I speak with new instructors, I sometimes ask how many of them would be happy if 20% or fewer students participated in discussion; some raise their hands. I raise the number to between 20 and 30, and many hands go up. Between 30 and 40, the numbers begin to dwindle, and by the time I ask how many would expect 80% to 90% to speak in class, not one hand casts a shadow. But why? There is no reason not to expect every single student to participate. Easier said than done, of course, but having full participation is not at all impossible.

Introduce the topic of class participation by talking with students about the purposes of discussion in college classes. On one hand, it is about reinforcing their learning and their understanding of the content of the course and about encouraging them to question the propositions being put forth. On the other hand, the *process* of a discussion class is designed to offer practice in speaking—in engaging in public, academic discourse, to be more precise. You might add that when students leave college behind and go into the world of work—no matter where it is—clear communication is one of the most valued skills. Their employers will expect them to be articulate speakers (the interview is the first big test, and if a student fails that, he or she won't get the job).

Telling your students that you expect 100% participation in discussions is another way to set up the expectation. Assignments such as the "go-round" (see chapter 8, p. 109) or those that require every student to bring in a question or a quotation from their homework can provide natural ways to achieve full participation.

By structuring experiences where everyone speaks, you can forestall that social situation that many of us have been in, whether in a classroom or at a dinner party, where some naturally dominant people who are easy conversationalists talk and talk and talk. Their "wait time" between comments is shorter than the average wait time, and they comfortably jump in with their stories. If you are not one of these speakers, you know what it feels like to have the minutes pass, more and more of them, without contributing anything yourself. Before too long, you find yourself feeling like a tongue-tied observer, and when someone finally gets around to addressing you, you can barely spit out a response.

A responsible leader of a group, or host of a party, will make sure that all people present feel welcome. A fundamental way to encourage and enable this full exchange is to use a discussion technique that gives each person an opportunity to participate, to speak up, to have his or her comments listened to and perhaps commented on, to receive eye contact from others, and to be granted membership in the group.

I was at a conference once where an educator presented a session on this elemental human need to belong. She sent five people out of the room and put the rest of us into five groups. While the five individuals were gone, she told the groups to stand in tight, closed circles and talk about a designated topic; we were to completely ignore the people who would try to join our groups. She brought the outsiders in and told each one of them to join one of the groups, and each one tried to gain access but was totally rebuffed. The activity went on for about five minutes before she called "time" and let the outsiders know what was going on in the exercise. Her revelation about the purpose of the activity (being inclusive) did not alleviate the hard feelings she had created in those who were the guinea pigs and some of those who felt complicity with her experiment. One woman left the session in tears, and many of the evaluations rated the exercise as excessively harsh. People need to be treated respectfully, and we hurt when we are not.

Creating Guidelines *With* Students

Instructors often expect to take full responsibility for energizing class discussion, but in fact the students can be part of this planning by having a class discussion about discussions. An effective method to use here is to have students form small groups during one of the first few classes and ask them to talk about the best and worst discussions they have participated in. One student can list good attributes, one can list bad, and then they can write the lists on the board. (This activity itself demands high participation.)

Topics that are likely to come up include a lively atmosphere and positive, respectful group dynamics. Negative experiences might include dominating people or those who offer remarks that are intolerant or mocking or embarrassing. The points students raise will remain a touchstone to use throughout the term. Depending upon your discipline and your course, attributes of a good discussion may overlap with behavior guidelines (as discussed in chapter 4, p. 57–60).

Points you may want to raise if the students don't mention them include

- Political correctness: What it is, why it exists, is it political or is it respect?

- Discussing issues without intimidating or insulting your "opponent" and without feeling hurt if your point is disagreed with
- Ways to speak up when you feel shy or intimidated
- Public discourse in the media that consists of yelling, needling, interruptions, and one-upmanship illustrates language use and behavior that are not examples of informed debate or expression but rather serve primarily to provide entertainment
- The academy and the classroom are places where civilization advances; good conversation is a key element

This discussion will give everyone a common memory to draw from regarding what works and what doesn't, what is difficult, and what is important. At those moments where the process of the discussion goes awry, you can pause the action and remind the students of their list. You may find that students themselves will bring it up.

A Safe Environment

One of your responsibilities as an instructor is to make the classroom safe for talk. Safe doesn't mean that there won't be controversy, and it doesn't mean that people will not disagree with each other, but it ought to mean that people will feel they can venture ideas, express minority views, and disagree with others. The college classroom is the place to practice speaking, though as in other social situations, no one wants to look foolish or sound stupid. Discuss this aspect of discussion as often as it seems appropriate to do so.

One fall a new professor in her first year of teaching asked me to visit her class to give her a general assessment of how well things were going. The visit proved memorable for me, because during discussion *two* students felt emboldened to express the fact that they had a disagreement with the ideas being put forth but did not know how they could articulate exactly what they were thinking. This expressing of troubled thoughts in such a preformed state illustrated an ideal classroom environment. It is a rare environment where we feel safe enough to utter the words: "I want to say something about this topic, but I can't quite figure out how to express myself right now." The manner in which you establish discussion guidelines will help create this type of comfort level. In fact, you may have an opportunity to model the behavior for students if an unexpected idea comes up, and you make the kind of statement the students in that class made.

Classrooms, then, are an important venue for the practice it takes to become a confident, comfortable, and articulate speaker. They are places to learn how to consider and respond to others' viewpoints, to analyze facts and reanalyze them with new information, and to raise questions and formulate opinions. Learning this art is one of the reasons that students pay tuition; it doesn't hurt to remind them of that occasionally.

Learning Names—Everyone's Task

The importance of learning students' names cannot be overstated; analogies are everywhere. Imagine how you would feel if during an internship of 8, 10, or 13 weeks, your boss never remembered your name. I am speaking, of course, about classes of 18 to 25 or so.

Remember, too, that students should learn each other's names. The analogy above applies again, with the additional point that it would be very strange to be assigned to be part of a group of people for a period of time and not be introduced to one another. To promote the evolution of your class into a community of learners, a key foundation is that they be acquainted with each other. Active learning is far more effective when students know each other.

Instructors may be anxious about devoting time to learning names, but it can be done in small doses and will be well worth the trouble.

If you meet students only once a week or have 60 to 75 names to learn, I would strongly recommend using name cards. I taught a class that met weekly for a few hours, and the classroom had several tables instead of desks. I passed out stiff half-sheets of paper and markers on the first day, and I asked students to fold the sheet in half and put their names on both sides of it so that people next to them could see their name as well as those across from them. The students brought their name cards back to subsequent classes and after four or five sessions, everyone knew everyone else's name.

If your room has movable desks, bring tape and a bold marking pen to class. Ask students to tape file cards or half sheets displaying their names in bold ink to the front of the desks. If the desks are in a circle, it will be easy to see the names. Make a point of craning your neck, if need be, to see a name that is hidden. Students will catch on and make the same effort. Stiff placards on the floor in front of students will work, too.

Who Speaks and Who Doesn't and Who Talks Too Much

Many research findings over past decades have found females, by and large, to be less confident about speaking up in class. No doubt the women in the vanguard of the women's liberation movement as well as those who worked for so many years for women to acquire the right to vote expected each of their levels of progress to put men and women on an even playing field in communication, too, but it hasn't been so.

Changes have occurred, of course, but researchers continue to note that women express themselves in a different way and/or less often than men. Joyce Slochower, a faculty member in New York University's postdoctoral program in psychotherapy and psychoanalysis said, "Women are more likely to be anxious about the value of their ideas in the first place, while for men, the issue is how to deal with the competition" (Stone, 2001, paragraph 6). An author who has analyzed and described gender talk extensively is Deborah Tannen (e.g., 1990, 1994), whose publications explore the differences in how men and women speak in social situations and the power dynamics of formal and informal conversations. It is of course a generalization to say women hesitate to speak out, because many do so eagerly. And there are certainly men who hesitate to assert themselves, too. Furthermore, several factors beyond gender may inhibit a person from speaking up in a group: shyness, feeling new and perhaps alienated, the number of people in the group, fears about dialects or accents, intimidation—unwitting or even unconscious—by assertive members of the group, past experiences in classrooms, and so on. Instructors have the responsibility to create the optimum learning atmosphere for every student in class. Exercising respect and interest in each student is the place to begin. Learning names and employing active learning strategies are good ideas, too, since many of them foster ways to help students overcome hesitancy in speaking by requiring contributions in small groups.

If you have felt shy in a situation where a more authoritative person helped you assert yourself in a way that didn't embarrass you, you likely have a positive memory to draw on—a memory of feeling respected and of standing up for yourself or your ideas. We want students to have these experiences in college so that they can feel confident about taking their education into the world and participating confidently in work and social situations.

A common concern of new faculty members and new GSIs is the student who speaks too frequently or too long or both. If one or more of your students behave this way, steps must be taken to maintain the good spirit of the class. A strategy to use in the classroom is to drop eye contact with the student and even to move around in such a way that he or she is out of your direct vision. If these hints don't have an impact (and I always suspect that such hints have long been ignored by the speaker or he or she would have learned the social skill previously), you'll want to see the student outside class.

Meetings of this type can make new instructors anxious, but couch the conversation in terms of the enthusiasm the student is showing in class. These students obviously have a lot of interest and plenty to say on the content of the course, which is good. Then talk about the limited time you have with students in the classroom and that you want other students to have the opportunity to enter the discussion so they can express their ideas and practice improving their speaking skills. (It might be the case that other students rely on one or two to come prepared and carry the day, which is also no favor to the group.) There may be points from the class's initial discussion on discussion (see chapter 4, p. 58) that would be appropriate to raise, too. This chat can be quite painless, as long as the student feels his or her engagement in the course is appreciated. You may also want to ask such students not to raise their hands or speak up more than once or twice a class—at least for a while. With luck, the "while" will last long enough for the dynamics to shift.

Difficult or Challenging Topics: Taboos, Personal Values, and Hurt or Angry Feelings

Many courses cover topics that students feel personally connected to, either from experience or from their spiritual or political belief systems. Some "difficult topics" easily come to mind, such as abortion, evolution, affirmative action, national health care, immigration, and privacy issues. But the span of possibilities is much wider. You have no idea as you stand in front of a group of students if family or friends of your students have declared bankruptcy, committed suicide, divorced, died, or learned they have a terminal disease. You may have a student who was mugged or raped, and the pain of such experiences may be just under the surface, ready to cause a reaction while you are carrying on with course material.

You cannot anticipate every sensitive topic, and even if you could, the college classroom is no place to sidestep difficult discussions. What you can do is introduce the discussion of obviously controversial material with some meta-analysis. You can tell students that, for instance, racism is going to be discussed in a class on the Vietnam War, and that the descriptions of some ugly behaviors and language will be part of the discussion. Emphasize to students that a primary goal of higher education is to learn how to discuss these issues. Assure students that emotional reactions are inevitable, but it is important to learn how to talk about difficult topics. The learning in this case includes recognizing others' viewpoints and evaluating their validity, listening to critiques of one's own views, and developing ways to disagree. Introducing some of the challenges that may arise gives a preview to the topic and invites students to prepare themselves for how they might handle their personal reactions.

Another type of difficulty can arise from disagreement. Many students don't know how to argue a point in a reasoned way. They may become emotional or hold back for fear of hurting someone's feelings. As citizens of the world, educated people need to be able to discuss topics that matter deeply. Remind your students a few times during the term that college is a very good place to practice this challenging art. Chapter 8, "Facilitating Discussions," deals with this issue further and offers some practical methods to defuse the kinds of emotional outbursts that can vitiate any hope of holding a classroom conversation on a controversial topic.

Humor

Humor in the classroom has developed into a subtopic of teaching methods. Workshops, books, and articles are proliferating, even with amusing titles, such as Ronald A. Berk's *Professors Are From Mars, Students Are From Snickers* (2003). Keep in mind that it is not your job to be funny. While teaching contains aspects of performance, you are under no obligation to be a stand-up comedian, tell jokes, or make people laugh. Berk collects jokes and humorous tales and uses them with great success to maintain student interest. He reports findings from a 1997 survey of a quarter million students from

500 universities, where more than 35% reported that they "were frequently bored in class" (p. 77). The causes and cures for boredom are a complex topic. For new instructors, as you know, forced humor often backfires.

Although a certified joke rarely belongs in class material, regardless of what a peer might say, quips about content or the discipline can lighten a session and are completely appropriate. Humorous lines or analogies often arise naturally in the course of teaching. If you sense an appropriate comment at the edge of your mind and you've established a good rapport with your students, don't suppress the remark. Humor should be as welcome in the classroom as good lighting. Don't avoid it. When the opportunity arises, enjoy it. Laughter serves all kinds of good purposes and promotes esprit de corps.

Laughing at Others—Be Prepared

Students. It goes without saying that for a student to laugh at another student's effort is completely inappropriate. If students laugh at someone's answer, you must immediately rescue that student and everyone else by saying, for instance, "Wait, wait, wait a minute. That answer might make sense if you consider . . ." Neglecting a situation like that will cause discomfort for a lot of students.

You. If you do something that is funny or can be construed as being funny, say a few words to let students know they can laugh or at least smile. Such things seem inevitable in the classroom, whether it's a piece of chalk shattering into bits, a stack of books crashing to the floor, or an incorrect Web page appearing on the screen. Whatever pops into your head—"Well, the day is off to a good start"—or perhaps just an expression of helplessness will give students a clue that you may be embarrassed, but you aren't going to make matters worse by pretending that nothing happened. They won't mind seeing you as another fallible human.

While there is no way to completely prepare for the many types of discussions you want to have or the many blunders, large or small, that occur in a classroom where people are communicating, it can be of some help to consider the issues that have been raised. You will learn a lot from your peers as the years pass. The good and bad moments of others will help you continue to build your own storehouse of knowledge regarding the way you plan discussions.

Preparing Content

Beyond preparing for the dynamics of discussion comes the meat of the matter: preparing content. In your first course and perhaps later ones, too, you may want to write out questions or citations you want to use. Experienced instructors may work from a brief list of topics either written out or in their heads, but new teachers will bring more clarity to a discussion and feel more confidence in their teaching if they write things down. Any single class can easily raise tangential questions and issues to attend to along with your plan, but having the plan will give you practical and psychological assurance.

Another reason to write out questions is to avoid the common experience of asking students a question, but as soon as you utter the question you think of a better way to ask it and you rephrase it. Sometimes this second question is followed by a third. All three of them are the same essential question or sometimes the three questions are in the same neighborhood. Imagine the listener's mind, or recall the experience yourself. When we hear a question, we begin to formulate a response or at least begin to wonder if we have enough information to form an answer. When a second question is layered on top of the first, we don't instantly wipe our minds clear; instead, we begin working on the second question, too. And so on. With so much brain activity going on in students' heads, either no one will speak or the discussion will get off to a muddy start. Writing questions down in advance eliminates this problem.

After asking a question, wait ten seconds for a student response. Instructors obviously have lots of thoughts regarding any question they ask, but when students hear a question, their minds scramble through the memories of notes they've taken, problems they've stewed over, or lectures they've heard as they select and shape their thoughts into a coherent response. It all takes time, though ten seconds seems like a long wait time in this culture. Some students may begin to worry that you are angry. The solution is to practice a silent period of ten seconds early in the course so everyone knows what it feels like, and then instead of fretting, they'll spend the time thinking.

An alternative strategy for discussion is not to ask a question. Instead, show a quotation, equation, or other aspect from their homework or from supporting material. Begin the discussion by talking about ways to consider what's on the screen or board. Or bring in a recent, relevant news story, a video clip (fiction or nonfiction), or an object—something that puts everyone on the same page as a starting point.

Additional suggestions for student-centered ways to use content are covered in chapter 8 on discussions and in chapter 9 on assignments.

Session Goals

One way to make active use of your class preparation is to use session goals. They allow you to guide the students, who may enter the room with their own minds full of distractions of all sorts, into your plan for the day.

As you plan a session, write a few notes that summarize your goals for the hour, and when you arrive, write them on a corner of the board. The goals may be about process:

- Review problems
- Read quotations from text
- Exchange drafts

Or they may be about content:

- Botticelli—bio
- Deconstruction defined
- Enron's use of Arthur Anderson Accounting Firm

When students can see a few words on the board about what will happen and who or what will be discussed, the sense of vagueness they had when they entered will dissipate and they can pull their attention to the topics at hand. A brief list of goals is the equivalent of an orchestra conductor tapping the baton on the music stand to bring the musicians to attention.

A second use of session goals concerns tempo. As the minutes pass, you can guide the session along by pointing to the board and reminding students you want to stay on track, if you do. An alternative use can occur if the class becomes completely absorbed in a topic and brain cells are nearly crackling under the stimulation. The last thing you may want to do is cut off the discussion. Instead, at the end of the class, note the fact that an item or two remain on the list and that you'll be dealing with them during the next session. This list benefits all the students by offering a road map for the hour, and it adds to your authority in the classroom because you are seen as being a competent navigator of the material. Even though discussion of some of the items is postponed, most students will appreciate your responsiveness as a teacher who bends the agenda to respond to engaged learners.

Using PowerPoint

This ubiquitous presentation software may or may not be right for you. It offers enormous advantages in and out of the classroom. Specifically, its linear structure has been found useful to instructors as they prepare classes and helpful to students in following the instructor's remarks. Like most technology, however, every advantage is matched by a distraction. Clifford Nass, who teaches at Stanford, confesses that he ended up removing a textbook from his course, a book that he thought was extremely valuable and rich, because he could not successfully turn its content into PowerPoint slides for his lecture (Parker, 2001).[1]

The major benefits of PowerPoint are that it allows you to prepare visuals, such as animations or multicolored graphs or charts, that would be much too tedious or impossible to show with conventional, older classroom technology, and it allows you to make one point at a time rather than distracting viewers with points you have not reached yet. AutoContent Wizard, a feature that supplies templates in PowerPoint, and whose name was a joke among the developers, does in fact offer welcome help to anxious presenters who are forced to insert session topics in a structured order.

Studies show that students feel the use of PowerPoint enhances their learning (Haugland, 1998), but there are also findings that students think that it "makes bad teachers worse" (paragraph 8) and that teachers who use it "speed up" (paragraph 7) their presentations (Smith, 2002). Perhaps a whole range of reactions can be found regarding the use of PowerPoint. The heart of the matter is that if you can make it work well for you and your students, then use it.

Beware, though, of a couple of disadvantages of PowerPoint (or any similar visual program). Lights often need to be turned down to make the pro-

---

[1] Nass, who worked at Intel prior to his academic career said, "What PowerPoint does is very efficiently deliver content [to students] . . . a lot more information—not just facts but rules, ways of thinking, examples" (paragraph 36). But he laments, "What you miss is the process. The classes I remember most, the professors I remember most, were the ones where you could watch how they thought. You don't remember what they said, the details. It was 'What an elegant way to wrap around a problem!' PowerPoint takes that away. PowerPoint gives you the outcome, but it removes the process" (paragraph 37).

jected images visible. There is a great deal of anecdotal information about students losing attention or going to sleep when lights are lowered, and it's no wonder: Humans are wired to go to sleep when rooms darken (National Institute of Health, n.d.). A second disadvantage is that the screen often becomes too dominant. GSIs and professors alike would do well to heed the words of Patrick Winston (1999), Ford Professor of Artificial Intelligence and Computer Design at Massachusetts Institute of Technology, who says that "You [the instructor] are the main course." All props and displays should support what you are saying. You are the live one here, with facial expressions and body language, a voice that grows softer and louder, a cadence that slows to emphasize words, and the power to make eye contact with students.

Ian Parker (2001), professor of neurobiology and behavior at the University of California at Irvine, reinforces this idea. "This is the most common complaint about PowerPoint. Instead of human contact, we are given human display" (paragraph 28).

A few strategies can help make the use of PowerPoint successful for your class.

- Be sure to adjust your slides—legible colors, font style, and type size—to the room you will be teaching in. For a room up to 40 feet long, 24 point is the recommended type size (*PowerPoint FAQ*).
- Use PowerPoint for a few minutes to make a point and then turn it off. Turn it on and off as needed to keep it from becoming the central focus in the classroom.
- Inform your students about the level of information they should expect to see on the slides. Tell them if you will be showing complex diagrams or equations that might be available on your Web site and that they should print out prior to class. Will you type only bullet headings? Would they be sufficient reminders for studying or do you want students to add their own notes?

In thinking about the ways that PowerPoint assists instructors, Parker (2001) says, "It helps you make a case, but it also makes its own case: about how to organize information, how much information to organize, how to look at the world" (paragraph 5). Edward Tufte (2003), professor emeritus of political science, statistics, and computer science at Yale University, who has examined the power of visual representation of information extensively, is another outspoken critic of PowerPoint and the ways it can edit our thoughts or influence the very manner in which we think about things.

A journalism professor I know used PowerPoint for about one quarter of a term. Looking out over his students, class after class, and seeing them sit numbly staring at the screen and not taking notes, he decided to stop using the program. Some students reacted with outrage. Lectures for them meant PowerPoint, and they didn't think it was "fair" for him not to use it. What is fair in college is for instructors to stretch students' minds. Teachers should feel free to experiment with a variety of methods to do precisely that.

The bottom line with PowerPoint is that you need to decide when and if it is appropriate for your class. If it serves the interests of improving student learning, then using it is the right choice.

References

Berk, R. A. (2003). *Professors are from Mars, students are from Snickers*. Sterling, VA: Stylus.

Haugland, J. (1998). *Using computer technology and course Web pages to improve student performance in accounting courses*. Retrieved August 10, 2006, from http://www.mtsu.edu/~itconf/proceed98/jhaugland.html

National Institute of Health, National Center on Sleep Disorders Research. (n.d.) *Sleep, sleep disorders, and biological rhythms*. Retrieved August 10, 2006, from http://science.education.nih.gov/supplements/nih3/sleep/guide/info-sleep.htm

Parker, I. (2001, May 8). Absolute PowerPoint: Can a software package edit our thoughts. *The New Yorker*. Retrieved May 15, 2006, from http://www.physics.ohio-state.edu/~wilkins/group/powerpt.html

PowerPoint FAQ. Authors hidden. Retrieved August 10, 2006, from http://www.rdpslides.com/pptfaq/

Smith, G. (2002). Student perceptions of technology in the classroom: The good, the bad, and the ugly. *ATLAS Ameritech/ACI, Teaching, Learning, and Sharing*. Retrieved August 10, 2006, from http://faculty.mckendree.edu/ATLAS/student_perceptions.htm

Stone, E. (2001, March 27). Examining, and easing, the anxiety of authorship. *The New York Times*. Retrieved December 1, 2007, from http://query.nytimes.com/gst/fullpage.html?res=9E0DE2DC113CF934A15750C0A9679C8B63&fta=y

Tannen, D. (1990). *You just don't understand: Women and men in conversation*. New York: William Morrow.

Tannen, D. (1994). *Talking from 9 to 5: Women and men at work: How women's and men's conversational styles affect who gets heard, who gets credit, and what gets done at work*. New York: William Morrow.

Tufte, E. (2003, September). PowerPoint is evil. Power corrupts. PowerPoint corrupts absolutely. *Wired, 11*(9). Retrieved May 15, 2006, from http://www.wired .com/wired/archive/11.09/ppt2.html

Winston, P. (1999). *How to speak: Lecture tips from Patrick Winston*. Derek Bok Center for Teaching and Learning at Harvard University [Video, 2nd ed.]. (Available from Derek Bok Center for Teaching and Learning, Harvard University, Science Center 318, One Oxford Street, Cambridge, MA 02138–2901)

8

FACILITATING DISCUSSIONS

Discussions generally center on **Texts, Problems, and Evidence** related to course content, whether faculty members or GSIs instigate the conversation directly or whether they **Rely on Homework** tasks to spark discussion. Your decisions about ways to run discussions will be enhanced once you see **What You Should Know About How Well Students Read**. After the topics are in focus, you need to consider whether technology use will enhance instruction and if so, how. Although it may be obvious to some, opportunities in **Using the Board** to initiate, guide, or push discussion should not be neglected because of the dominance of PowerPoint. Other modes of technology, including **Video Clips and Films,** can also facilitate discussion classes, and so, of course, can assignments **Using Computer Displays and Overheads**.

Instructors can use a wide variety of **Formats to Jump-Start Discussions**, including **Go-Round, Four Corners, Elephant, Fishbowl, Jigsaw, Debates—Instant and Others**. Sometimes classes seem to go slack, and you may want to call a **Time-Out for Sluggish Sessions**. The opposite case, **Discussions Gone Wild**, can make use some of the same basic techniques. A final aspect of teaching that faculty and GSIs can expect to experience at some point is the necessity of **Dealing With Un(der)prepared Classes**; several options are suggested, some of which might serve all of your classes well.

E ffective discussions demand good planning. Instructors must prepare a design for the discussion. The plan may involve a series of questions or some printed material or selections from homework. Students, too, must come prepared. That preparation may involve homework or it may simply be a willingness to engage in the propositions put forth by their teachers.

Some key points for running successful discussions were included in chapters 3, 6, and 7. Here is a brief summary of some tips:

- Arrange the room so that students can see each others' faces.
- Learn students' names and continue to offer two- or three-minute exercises that allow students to learn each other's names. (Any group activity can begin by students introducing themselves to one another.)
- Write out questions in advance.
- Prepare a backup plan, such as accumulating file cards with questions, quotations, or jargon that you could use with pairs or small groups for a spontaneous review session during sluggish days.
- Remember to use the 10-second rule after you ask a question.
- If silence occurs mid-discussion simply because some thought-provoking propositions have been put forth, you could say, "Let's let these notions settle in our minds for a minute or two before moving on." Silence can have its place in a discussion, and it often leads to an even richer continuing conversation.
- Move around the room to help shift the focus away from one location, and encourage students to speak to each other, not just you.

Texts, Problems, Evidence

The "stuff" of education generally hinges on solving problems of one sort or another through texts (including visual and aural ones), formulas, or physical evidence of some kind. The activities that support problem solving may include summarizing what is known, plucking highlights from masses of material, examining or reexamining physical evidence, applying values to symbols in a complex equation, or scrutinizing some aspect of a text. An exercise that begins from an unusual or a narrow viewpoint or that focuses on a case study may expand into rich classroom conversations about larger issues.

One way to keep discussions lively is to alter the pace of class time or to introduce new formats from time to time. The following activities have a degree of spontaneity.

- Assign pairs to examine X page or paragraph, Y graph, the introduction or the conclusion, and report back on their findings.

- Ask pairs to explore questions, such as: "What do the authors want you to think about?" "What are the authors trying to prove; how successful is it?"
- If you want them to attend to the form or process, ask them to look at vocabulary and jargon, to unpack an argument, or to create a method of illustrating data.
- Entice students into engaging with fresh subjects by creating activities that invite them to grapple with new ideas or information *before* the assigned material has been read. Like the preknowledge survey (see p. 70 in chapter 5), an activity that provokes students into thinking and wondering about unknown or little known information can be a highly effective and helpful door into the subject.
- Give small groups an assignment that needs to be illustrated—a problem to be solved, a flow chart, a hierarchy—and appropriate tools to do their work, which might be a laptop or colored pens and a clean transparency. After the groups have filled in the information, let them give a brief presentation explaining their thinking.

Relying on Homework

Students can be asked to prepare some triggers to seed discussions. Depending upon the request, you may want to leave the choices as open-ended requests or assign sections that they should draw from. Ask them to bring to class

- a single-paragraph response to designated material
- three questions on some matter
- an imitation of a problem or a poem
- a quotation from the text with a brief comment about it
- a summary or review of designated text
- three historical events or three attributes of a character in a book or play or of figures or concepts

These assignments could be dealt with in small groups, exchanged with other pairs of students for discussion, or the material might be used for a group to construct a graphic design that connects the items.

What You Should Know About How Well Students Read

If you use only one other book to aid you in your teaching, my strong recommendation is John C. Bean's (1996) *Engaging Ideas: The Professor's Guide to Integrating Writing, Critical Thinking, and Active Learning in the Classroom*. Bean offers a collection of research on how college students read (not as well as we or they imagine they do) and how to help them.

In a study that underscores the need to work on reading abilities, the National Assessment of Adult Literacy, sponsored by the National Center for Education Statistics, under the U.S. Department of Education, tested 19,000 adults (out of the 26.4% of college graduates in the country) who had graduated from college by 2003 and found that less than a third (31%) could read at a high level, that is, they were able to draw inferences from lengthy, complicated prose. Three percent could not even perform at a basic level—locating an easily identified piece of information in a short piece of text. The previous test, in 1992, found that 40% could perform at a high level, so the past decade has seen a remarkable and sad decline (Dillon, 2005).

There is often a crevasse between the level of writing in most high school textbooks and the sorts of books, journal articles, and original documents that students encounter in college, from CIA reports to U.S.-tribal treaties to literature of all sorts to schematics, instructions, or explanations for business, science, and engineering. When professionals write for other professionals, they are not thinking about high school students, and many texts used in college are, appropriately, aimed at the professional, experienced audience. It is no wonder that many students need some guidelines for their reading.

Challenges to Reading—It's Harder Than They Think

Help students crack the codes that can lead to more accomplished reading. Bean (1996) lists commonly held assumptions that are barriers to students' learning to read well. At the top is students' belief that experts—GSIs, faculty, and professionals—read quickly and understand what they read. Since students are practicing to be experts, they read quickly, but they don't always understand it, and consequently they expect their instructors to explain the text. Therefore one important teaching strategy is to tell and show students how you read. Bring in a passage that you have grappled with, talk about the vocabulary and the sentence complexity and any underlying assumptions, explain how you unpacked it and then returned to it a few times before you understood it. Remind them of something in their past that they didn't get right away—geometry proofs and theorems, phases of the moon (truly—a lot of them may still not have it mastered; see the discussion on *A Private Universe* on p. 64 in chapter 5), symbolism in Faulkner's "The Bear," or another widely read story in their earlier education. The point is that learning is neither automatic nor subconscious. It is not simply a matter of unrolling a long rug with revelation upon revelation appearing like magic and leaping as fully comprehended material into the mind. Learning takes thinking and it takes time.

Strategies to Help Students Improve Reading

If you are requiring challenging reading—and sometimes the basic text for a class fits this criterion—select a representative few paragraphs, photocopy the text block, then trim and copy it again in such a way that the paragraphs are in the middle of the page with a large border of white around it. Invite students, individually or with partners, to "interact" with the text and write questions about words or concepts, about what the author seems to assume they already know, about puzzling conclusions that seem to be drawn or words that are new or used in unfamiliar ways. Doing this once, slowly and deliberately, will help students understand that reading can be arduous and demanding, and that they should be patient when they feel confused or when the text seems too dense to master in a single reading. I would suggest that you do the assignment, too, with as much detail as possible, and then display your page on an Elmo projector or pass it among the students.

Another idea is to introduce a book by discussing how the author leads readers into the material, how the chapters are laid out, and invite them to consider why the author and publisher chose the design, how well the index may serve them, and so on. This exercise varies by discipline and text, but by looking at the book as a college text and asking yourself and your students how it differs from a high school book on the same topic, some useful notions can emerge about how to approach a book, what should and should not be assumed, and methods for dealing with the differences. Textbook prose can not only seem impenetrable but sometimes—let's face it—it can be poorly written. Books by committees are more likely to contain prose that is passive and even murky, moving from one idea or event to another without adequate transitions, relying on assumptions about readers' knowledge that are inappropriate, or carrying other indications of having been pushed to publication too quickly (Schemo, 2006). Too often, the production itself becomes the project, with egos fighting for their turf. The needs of the audience may receive short shrift in the process. Mention to students that publication can be political, that not all texts are created equal. Even though information may be highly valuable, if the presentation is obtuse, despite glossy paper and a flashy layout, students are entitled to know that. If you have spotted particularly nasty sections or writing habits of the author(s), warn students—like watching for hazardous shallow places in a river. These things can be managed, but they need special attention.

A dictionary is an obvious aid, and students should use one—their own or one of the many available online (college libraries often have links on their home Web page or on the lead page for reference books).

Additional problems cited by Bean (1996) include students' inability to adjust their reading styles to the text at hand. Sometimes skimming is appropriate, and sometimes digging or rereading is called for. First-year students tend to treat words in an egalitarian way, giving each word and each sentence the same weight. If you follow the suggestion of introducing the book, look together at introductions and conclusions of chapters or of the whole book. When they are well done, these sections highlight important signposts to watch for. It's not cheating to read a conclusion first. Look, too, at sections that describe charts or graphs. If students can get the information they need by studying the graph, they should be told that they could simply skim accompanying prose; that is what experts would do. Attending to bold-faced headlines and first paragraphs, and skimming the rest of the section is obviously another good way to become familiar with the text before reading it thoroughly. These suggestions will help students begin to learn to read the way experts do.

Other reading challenges that Bean (1996) cites and describes include difficulties perceiving the structure of an argument, assimilating unfamiliar material, understanding rhetorical contexts, and tracking complex syntax. Students may also lack the cultural literacy that would allow them to connect to the text, or they may have an inadequate vocabulary. Clearly, it is no service to your students' learning or to their lives beyond school to ignore these problems.

When you discuss these matters with students, flip the issues into the positive mode so that you can talk about how much the average college student's vocabulary grows, how understanding of contexts and complex prose will rise, and so on, but these things don't happen instantly or with ease.[1] Putting issues like these on the table can help students bring up reading problems in class (for instance, when new articles are assigned), and students may also be more willing to e-mail you or to come to your office with questions. You might suggest that they communicate with their computer buddy or members of their small group, if you have designated these connections, about the texts, too.

Using the Board

Blackboards or white boards can be used in lots of creative ways as part of a discussion. Pairs or trios can

- work problems
- make lists
- write down evidence
- draw graphs, charts, or flow charts.

Sometimes you may want to begin class with board work, but some creative board activity provides a welcome break in the session, too. Having students work on the board can be a powerful way to share the authority of the session and raise student participation.

Video Clips and Films

Another form of media that GSIs and professors use in the classroom with more and more ease are films or video clips of movies, news programs, or special-interest topics. Nonfiction and fiction films can illustrate or embellish course content in an extremely helpful way. Nancy Hauserman, Williams Teaching Professor in the Tippie College of Business at the University of Iowa, teaches Introduction to Law. At the appropriate moment in a session on contract law, students suddenly find themselves viewing a clip from the 1992 comedy *My Cousin Vinny*. In the scene, Joe Pesci, as Vinny Gambini, stomps into a bar, approaches a big lout hanging over his beer, and demands that the fellow hand over $200. The money was an overdue payoff on a bet

---

[1] Unsurprisingly, there is disagreement about the estimates of words learned but not about the large growth of vocabulary itself.

the drinker had placed on a game of pool that he played and lost to Vinny's girlfriend. The big guy offers to beat Vinny up instead of paying the $200. Vinny responds: "Oh, you like to negotiate as you go along. We lawyers call that a counteroffer." And so it goes. End of clip. "That," says Hauserman, "is negotiation at work." Needless to say, students' attention comes to the fore at such an unexpected moment in class (N. Hauserman, personal communication, September 14, 2006).

Such an example illustrates two important things about the use of film in classrooms. One, GSIs can introduce a light moment from popular culture to illustrate serious concepts. Two, even the shortest clip can be effective in refocusing the dynamics within the classroom.

If you use film as an educational tool rather than just a prompt into other subjects, you should remind or inform your students that films are full of conventions. This fact is particularly important when you use film to illustrate a real event. Every film and every documentary has a producer and director. Everything about angle, composition, music, voice-overs, lighting, and, of course, the script and actors is carefully planned. A viewpoint is being presented along with the material.

Using Computer Displays and Overheads

Computer displays have taken the front row for classroom presentation for the same reason that they have become a standard tool for virtually every scholar. The wealth of information and animations, plus selected input, makes them ideal for the classroom. The keys to successful use is knowing how to use the appropriate software and having reliable technology on hand.

An overhead projector was once the PowerPoint of the classroom. Overheads still can provide a low-technology ease of use and may be ideal for some presentations. First, if you want to display only one or two pages of a static image or words, it will be easier to print a few acetate sheets rather than creating a PowerPoint show. This depends upon the content (an image may be available to photocopy, for instance, more easily than it can be accessed by means of a computer, or your classroom may not have the proper technology). Also, about the only thing that can go wrong with a projector is a blown-out bulb. Usually a spare one is kept with the machine.

The most common misuse of overheads—as is common with Power-Point slides—probably concerns putting too many words on one sheet. Students who scramble to discern the print and copy down the sentences may be missing important opportunities to listen or to participate.

A newer, and in some instances more convenient, version of overhead projection is the Elmo, which allows you to put a book or paper on a surface and project it as it appears on an overhead screen. Such a direct line between the desired image and the projected image could be a boon for many teaching purposes.

Some Formats to Jump-Start Discussions

Here are some suggestions for formal discussion structures that you will need to prepare for, though they could be introduced into class spontaneously. An unusual design can reenergize the class. There is no end to the possible variations on these strategies. Your material will likely spark ideas, as may conversations with peers. Even though the activities may be used in what students may perceive as an off-the-cuff manner, they need preparation. Most new instructors are hesitant to improvise.

Once you have used some learning activities with success, you will be able to initiate them more easily, and very likely you will eventually be able to use one on the spur of the moment. Sometimes unexpected turns (sharp disagreements, provocative questions or responses) in what had been a typical discussion can raise an opportunity for an unplanned activity. Some GSIs and faculty have exercised improvisational teaching moments in the past (through swimming lessons, coaching, parenting, and so on), and they are comfortable doing so in the classroom. If you haven't had experiences improvising with a group, start small and be brief. Your students will value the success as much as you will, and you'll gain the confidence to do it again.

Go-Round

This common method used for introductions, where students "go around" and introduce themselves can be used in a number of ways to serve learning goals and stimulate discussion. It can also often be done with minimal planning.

The obvious starting point is a question that will elicit a variety of responses. As students answer, write notes on the board in various categories, and then refer to the list as the discussion gets under way. If the question doesn't bring forth a range of answers, stop when that becomes evident and begin the discussion or ask the rest of the class a different question.

Another version of this exercise begins with giving students a few minutes to write. Ask students a question related to the reading or invite them to select a quotation from it. Collect the papers in a hat or other container and pass it around so students draw something out that they didn't write. They can then read the paper aloud and comment on it. Perhaps different aspects will surface that can be grouped to further the discussion. In a session begun this way you should not let these snippets float around as if they were fortunes from cookies. You will need to help students connect their thoughts so that a meaningful discussion results. This will happen quite readily if you have planned your questions well.

The great benefit of this discussion technique is that everyone talks, which not only encourages some of the quieter students to speak up but also prevents the overtalkers from dominating the floor. Many points will have been raised, so a lively discussion generally follows.

Some instructors keep this method in mind for use on a day when a class feels particularly sluggish. You may develop additional versions that suit your style and your discipline.

The Elephant

American poet John Godfrey Saxe's (1865) "The Blind Men and the Elephant" illustrates the pitfalls of having a lot of information about one aspect of a problem. In order to solve the problem, the group must share their evidence and rethink how to find the solution.

This activity structure might be adapted to many disciplines and subjects. One example is to use it as a prelearning event. Select five aspects of the upcoming topic, which might be the jet stream, infant mortality in sub-Saharan Africa, the music of Punjab, the characters in Ibsen's *Doll House*, or the density of various layers within Mount St. Helens. Separate the students into five groups and assign each group one aspect of the topic. To each of the extracted items, add some context and a question for the five groups to stew over. Students should then develop an argument for why their piece of information provides a basis for the most cogent line of reasoning. After they have time to reach a conclusion, invite a student from each group to summarize the discussion. It may be appropriate for the speakers to write the high points on the board.

The class as a whole can then discuss how the pieces fit together, which aspects of the arguments best fit together, and how to make the best case from the supplied information.

If an activity of this sort lasts even fifteen minutes, the students will leave the classroom with a lot of ideas about the material.

Four Corners

This activity works well at any point in the term and can breathe life into a day when energy is flagging. One approach is to offer a topic or question that allows people to take a stand on the central tenet—that they "strongly favor," "somewhat favor," "strongly oppose," or "somewhat oppose." These positions are assigned to locations in the room, and students are invited to go to the designated spot. This physical activity provides a good break.

Once in their corners, they should discuss their convictions or opinions so that they can agree that they are in the area they want to be in. If some students haven't decided how they feel, they should move from one place to another and listen and ask questions. After a few minutes, each group should be able to describe its stance.

An alternative way to divide the class into four (or whatever number suits your material) is to assign to each group a character from a novel or play, one section of the geologic time chart, players in a political or economic scandal or event, countries in a war, and so on. Again, each group can develop its response to a central question and then report to the class at large.

Debates

We generally think of debates as demanding lengthy preparation, deep research, and lots of file cards, but they don't need those features to provide good results. Nancy Hinman (2005) from the geosciences department at the University of Montana teaches a course in hydrochemistry in which students present a debate very early in the term. During the second week, halfway through her 90-minute session, Hinman breaks them into debate teams of three or four people. Students either defend or refute a statement about global warming; they must use science only, no policy. The students have the rest of that class, half of the one following, and if needed, one more half session to hammer out their arguments. She walks around the room and offers guidance, asking questions and evaluating their comments. Hinman says, "Even if they don't have all the answers, the activity gives them a purpose and they respond well." She adds, "Students like the way it gets them involved early in the semester" (N. Hinman, personal communication, February 9, 2007).

An "instant" debate offers an alternative way of having students endorse and explore one side or the other of an issue.

- Tell students to come to class ready to plan a team debate.
- Have them select a pro- or antiposition, so they can assemble in small groups and share their knowledge and ideas.
- Let them discuss their points for 15 minutes and then run debates for 10 minutes. In this way, everyone in a class of 24 would have the opportunity to prepare and present.

While debates are generally centered on unresolved issues, it may suit your course to ask students to explore a question (or questions) that has been settled. Could students expand their perspective on the content of your course by addressing questions such as: Should women vote? Is "bleeding" a good way to cure people? Can Goldbach's conjecture be solved? Should *The Scarlet Letter* be part of the American literary canon? Raising established attitudes or beliefs to be reexamined invites students to imagine or reintroduce a controversy and think more deeply about the arguments that lost and those that dominated the debate.

A good outcome for a debate occurs when students discover the limits of their knowledge and can say, "I wish I knew more about X, because then I could make an additional point." Make sure you tell students that this sort of contribution is welcome and valuable; you may even list such end points on the board and use them as a jumping-off place for an assignment.

Role-Playing

While this activity is often undertaken in drama classes, it can be effective in courses as dissimilar as finance or art history. Create a scenario that suits the topic. List the key players, bringing in, for instance, wealthy investors, someone who will suffer as a result of a particular decision, a central character (a painter of a particular piece, a leader whose thoughts are relevant in the deliberations—Sigmund Freud, Dmitri Shostakovich, Bill Gates, Sandra Day O'Connor, or whoever will spice up the mix for you), and a "journalist" who is reporting on the process and will ask probing questions and seek clarification.

Adopting a role, like donning a costume, often extends creative thinking. While the actors are fulfilling their parts, the audience can watch for good or faulty arguments and prepare questions to ask the actors—while they are still in their roles or as students reflecting on their roles.

Role plays can be an effective teaching tool, but they are also complex. A lot of unexpected opinions can crop up that may need to be addressed later in the class. As you create your scenario and select characters, define the central questions so that the scope is not too large. Set a time limit that allows players to exercise their characters, but leave sufficient time after the activity for viewers and players to react to what happened and for summation or closing comments.

Fishbowl

In a fishbowl discussion half the class or a group of up to a dozen sits in a circle to discuss a designated topic, and the other half of the class sits outside, making a second circle, observing. Variations abound, including assigning roles to people. You can also allow (or require) audience members to tap the shoulder of someone in the inner circle and swap places. You can also call a time-out periodically and let the inner and outer circles confer before resuming the inner discussion.

While the discussion is still lively, switch the speakers with the audience and allow a fresh group to carry it forward.

Mini-presentations

While major presentations are often a big project for students, mini-presentations are good practice and can be done in a number of ways. As you introduce a new subject area—piece of literature, cloud types, or competing theorists in your field—one version might go like this:

Let's say you have 21 students in a section.

- Prepare a sheet with seven numbered subtopics, each one described in a short paragraph.
- Put students into three groups and assign them numbers one to seven. Before giving them material—so you have their attention—describe

what they are to do and how long each segment will last, as described below.

- Hand out the sheets and tell students to use their numbers to see which paragraph they should read. They need to read it a few times and figure out how to tell their peers the substance of the information. Give them two minutes to prepare.

- Then, going around the circle, let each student present his or her summary in 30 seconds.

- Be a conscientious timekeeper to keep the circle on schedule. You want to follow the structure as closely as possible to maintain the "mini" aspect of the exercise and to keep from undercutting one of the values, which is to be able to summarize things well and briefly.

Jigsaw

This activity also uses small groups as instructional peer units, but the activity requires homework, so it needs to be preplanned. You may even want to build it into your syllabus. It can be especially valuable if there is an abundance of material you want students to read. For this example, let's say you have 25 students in your class, and let's say further that you'd like to enhance students' learning about a topic by having them know about five case studies that use nuances of the topic. If you cannot add the needed study time to their homework load, the jigsaw could provide a solution.

Divide the students into five groups of five, and assign each group its own case study. At the designated class, ask the groups to gather for a few minutes so they can review what they have all read and agree on the salient points. At this point, you need to reassemble the groups. Have the members of each group count off from one to five. Then reassemble the groups with all the "ones" in one group together, the "twos" in another, and so on. When these groups form, they should consist of five people who have each read a different case study. Now comes their task: Each person describes the case study he or she read and highlights the notable points. The other students take notes and ask questions. Plan the exercise so that students know how much time they should use in their presentations. Mark time for them, so that everyone has the opportunity to participate, and leave a few minutes at the end for summary and noting of highlights.

This activity may well take most of an hour-long session, but consider the multiple benefits to the students compared to, for instance, your lecturing about the case studies. This student-centered activity presses students to do close reading, design an appropriate summary, and select the most important points in an article. Then in class the students give presentations to a small group and respond to questions, then agree on larger themes.

The jigsaw offers a fine example of active learning. You can easily alter the variables to suit your discipline or course material. The method would be helpful for exposing students to original government documents, for instance, to paintings by a particular painter, buildings from a specified area, attributes of the Adiantaceae family of ferns, and so on. If students have a challenging chapter to comprehend, they may be assigned to read all of it, but sections could be parceled out to groups for the same treatment. Finally, if your number of students does not fit the example, you can simply have more than one "expert" in a group, and the pair can give the presentation.

Time-Outs for Sluggish Sessions

We forget that the popular sports tool, the time-out, can serve college classrooms as well. One place to use it is in the middle of dead silence—those sessions when *no one is saying anything*.

Few teaching situations are worse than a roomful of people where only one or two people speak again and again, or worse—when nobody says a word. Every question you pose falls into an abyss of silence. The absence of talk begins to feel like an absence of thought, and it develops its own life so that it becomes anathema to speak. You find yourself talking and talking, when what you had wanted was a *class* discussion.

You or someone you know may have been in a class where that has occurred, and the instructor responded by growing incensed and sending everyone away. There are alternatives.

Try humor. Or you could call a time-out and alter the way class is being conducted.

Tell students to pair off or form small groups and give them a specific assignment. They could discuss one of the questions that you've heard no response to. If students have not read their assignments (we'll deal with this in a moment), they may still have some thoughts to share. If they have done the homework but feel hesitant about speaking out, the low-risk atmosphere of a small group is easier to flounder around in than the full class.

If students have not been answering your questions about how to solve a problem, ask them to take a sheet of paper and work the problem as far as they can. Then they can compare their answers with a partner to see whether they agree. Ask pairs or groups of students to go to the board. If your room has enough board space, send all the groups to the board. Ask them to write on the board what they have on one of the sheets of paper, and from there on involve the whole class. Use this idea in a document-driven course by asking students to write down a puzzling or interesting quotation or problem from the text and have them put some of those on the board.

Another idea is to pass out file cards and ask each student to write down a word or phrase or line or two from an equation in response to the material. Collect the cards, shuffle them, and hand them to other students, who might then go into small groups to discuss the written notes.

Any of these methods of time-outs can shift the dynamics of the class. After a span of time with a fresh format, the mood may be such that the rest of the session will proceed with students reengaged. If not, consider adapting the action from the following story, or consult with your teaching supervisor, faculty peers, or department chair.

I was in a graduate class once when several weeks into the course it became obvious that only three or four of us contributed regularly. The class had fewer then 20 students, so it became awkward to speak up for the third or fourth time in the hour, but those of us who talked felt a tacit obligation to keep things moving forward. One day, midclass, the professor asked everyone to take out a sheet of paper and write something about the topic under discussion. We all did so. Then she said, "I see that all of you have written something about our text, so you all have thoughts about the essay we're discussing. But some of you do not contribute. Why is this?"

What followed was a discussion about the class. Some students expressed their uncertainties and so on. This sort of time-out can feel stressful because it pulls back the curtain on teaching in a way that is rarely done. But the outcome was a much-improved atmosphere with much freer conversation. This sort of action is similar to what happens in a relationship after one person says, "We need to talk."

Discussions Gone Wild

Sometimes it happens that classes erupt. Such a situation is well portrayed on the videotape *Race in the Classroom: The Multiplicity of Experience* (Derek

Bok Center for Teaching and Learning, 1992). Students from several ethnic and national backgrounds are asked by their instructor to discuss affirmative action. Personal experiences and beliefs soon join with resentment that leads to chaos. In a voice-over, the instructor leading the class expresses a sense of being completely overwhelmed.

Instructors cannot always foresee or prevent incendiary behavior—and some instructors like to see it happen. If you prefer to avoid such events, plan well for sessions that will include controversial topics. As part of your preparation, think about the biases or standpoints you yourself react to strongly so that you can prepare ways of responding if students express what might be volatile viewpoints.

You might begin class by discussing the challenges of conducting an emotion-free conversation about the issue and invite students to comment on why such topics might cause vitriolic responses. But if you have a class that erupts, declare a time-out. Stopping the action gives people a chance to breathe and be quiet for a few minutes. Then, depending upon the topic and source of the outbreak, take the next step.

Lee Warren (2002) advises that these events can turn into deep learning experiences if instructors (a) manage themselves and their responses and (b) locate and make use of the learning opportunity that the outburst presents. A time-out will help pull everyone away from the emotional heat. Once that is accomplished, the instructor can invite reflections on the issues that sparked such reactions and lead students toward considering others' points of view. Sometimes the classroom dynamics have echoed elements of the controversy itself. As challenging as it may be, the important point is not to ignore what has happened. The class, as a learning community, needs to address the difficulties, and students need to begin to approach new understandings about the content and the human interactions that occurred.

Some immediate strategies are to ask students to write for a few minutes. Perhaps you'll want to slow down the emotions by writing points on the board. Depending upon how out of control things become, a brief break would be a good idea. Warren (2002) suggests that an appropriate way to pull the conversation away from the flash point is to say, "'Many people think this way. Why do they hold such views? What are their reasons?' and then, 'Why do those who disagree hold other views?'" (2002, paragraph 16).

What you should *not* do is dismiss class. The hard but necessary task is to talk about what happened. Step out of the material itself and discuss the process with students. Eruptions can provide occasions for learning, but they demand unpacking—Why did the emotions explode? What facts do we know about the topic? How can we use this new knowledge to understand the subject better and keep from attacking or feeling attacked?

Most classrooms never experience complete meltdowns, but time-outs, which can be used in a variety of circumstances and are particularly useful in these situations, should be part of your teaching armamentarium.

Dealing With Un(der)prepared Classes

If you arrive in class one day to find that virtually no one has read the assignment, what will you do? Some students may expect you to dismiss them in a huff—a not uncommon reaction but one that means the whole hour is lost.

One alternative solution is to declare 10 or 15 minutes of silence while students read or attend to part of the task they were supposed to have done. You don't need to say a single scolding word; they will be well aware that they should have prepared *prior* to class. This plan salvages at least a portion of the session.

A second method of dealing with a lack of preparation is to focus together on one or two problems or on one section of the text. This can be done with the whole class or by splitting the class in half or into smaller groups.

Over time, you will find that there are seemingly endless ways of running discussions. Stephen Brookfield (Brookfield & Preskill, 1999) has devoted a great deal of study to using discussion in the classroom, as has Chris Christenson (Christenson, Garvin, & Sweet, 1992). Their books or other resources at your faculty development office will add to your strategies.

References

Bean, J. C. (1996). *Engaging ideas: The professor's guide to integrating writing, critical thinking, and active learning in the classroom.* San Francisco: Jossey-Bass.

Brookfield, S., & Preskill, S. (1999). *Discussion as a way of teaching: Tools and techniques for democratic classrooms.* San Francisco: Jossey-Bass.

Christensen, C. R., Garvin, D. A., & Sweet, A. (1992). *Education for judgment: The artistry of discussion leadership.* Cambridge, MA: Harvard Business School Press.

Derek Bok Center for Teaching and Learning, Harvard University (Producer). (1992). *Race in the classroom: The multiplicity of experience* [Videotape]. Coproduced with the Harvard Office for Race Relations and Minority Affairs. (Available from the Derek Bok Center for Teaching and Learning, Harvard University, Science Center 318, One Oxford Street, Cambridge, MA 02138–2901)

Dillon, S. (2005, December 16). Literacy falls for graduates from college, testing finds. *The New York Times*. Retrieved January 30, 2007, from http://www.ny times.com/2005/12/16/education/16literacy.html

Hinman, N. (2005). Geochemical debates. *On the Cutting Edge*. Retrieved February 6, 2007, from http://serc.carleton.edu/NAGTWorkshops/geochemistry/activi ties/9207.html

Saxe, J. G. (1865). *Clever stories of many nations/rendered in rhyme*. Boston: Ticknor and Fields.

Schemo, D. J. (2006, July 13). Schoolbooks are given F's in originality. *New York Times*. Retrieved December 2, 2007, http://www.nytimes.com/2006/07/13/ books/13textbook.html

Warren, L. (2002). *Managing hot moments in the classroom*. Derek Bok Center for Teaching and Learning, Harvard University. Retrieved January 3, 2007, from http://isites.harvard.edu/fs/html/icb.topic58474/hotmoments.html

9

PLANNING ASSIGNMENTS

Opportunities for Creating Assignments depend upon course responsibilities, which is particularly wide ranging for GSIs. To make assignments as effective as possible, **The Mechanics of Planning** help connect course goals to assigned tasks. While the availability of media is altering some kinds of homework, many tasks still use **Papers, Real and Cyber**.

In creating assignments, an important duality to consider is **Exercise Versus Display**—are students working with material to learn it, or are they demonstrating what they know? Beyond the assignments themselves, it is beneficial to understand some aspects of **Motivation** as well as the cognitive purposes of **Repetition**. Students benefit from this knowledge, too. Despite all good intentions and knowledge about teaching and learning, instructors still must rely, from time to time, on **Carrots and Sticks to Get Students to Do Their Homework**.

Assignments—large or small—between lectures, readings, and other instructional routines, provide a key method for taking stock in a course. They give instructors a chance to ask questions that probe students' grasp of big issues or important details. They give students the opportunity to reflect on, select, and use the knowledge they have acquired to display or grapple with displaying what they have learned.

Your Opportunities for Creating Assignments

New faculty members, of course, are responsible for creating all assignments. GSIs may have no role in preparing formal assignments, but course professors may ask you or welcome your request to develop informal assignments. Smaller assignments can help students keep up with course work, create opportunities for active learning, and generally raise the level of engagement during sessions.

Since those of us who teach in higher education have taken hundreds of courses and completed thousands of assignments, we have a repertoire to draw from. The vast majority of those assignments fit into three categories: writing papers, doing problems, and giving presentations, with technology offering more variety in their execution. All three activities serve the purpose of exercising the ability to use knowledge, but all three can be employed in more creative ways than they typically have been.

The Mechanics of Planning

Look at the calendar for your course, at the pace of topics, and required readings. Make a list of some active learning techniques you want to use during the term, and match material to activity. Any overall plan will likely shift as the weeks pass, but having a plan in place will give you a sense of peace and confidence as you proceed.

In the chapters on discussion, you saw several small assignments that work very well for accountability. As mentioned previously, for instance, if you ask students to copy a quotation or a portion of text or a problem onto a file card before class, the cards can be pooled and drawn out by other students for an activity. Even such a small assignment will have students attending to your course material. The class activities you can develop from this small process are plentiful: pairings, debates of various sorts, textual examinations, board work, and so on. Variety in assignments and activities will be a big boost in keeping your class energized.

Papers, Real and Cyber

New instructors will discover ways to improve their organization as each year of teaching passes, picking up ideas from peers about managing the materials of teaching and learning. Here are a few tricks that may already be part of your repertoire. If they're unfamiliar, consider giving them a try.

Handing papers back to students takes valuable classroom time, but before you adopt a method to avoid it, you should know that faculty and GSIs have said that they used the distribution of papers to learn or reinforce their knowledge of students' names as well as having a few seconds of personal contact with students. At the beginning of a course, especially, hand papers back. As the weeks pass, try some other methods.

Folders

Don't underestimate the use of colors, elementary though it may seem. Color provides instant recognition (file folders and plastic sheaths of many colors are sold at office supply stores and perhaps at your institution's bookstore). Assign one family of colors to each course or section.

Multiple folders can also be used to advantage in classes, large ones especially, where papers are collected and handed back frequently. If you are a grader for a professor, offer this idea to him or her to facilitate the mechanical dimensions of the task. Select four folders and assign each one to a section of the alphabet (use a bold black marker on the outside and inside of the front cover). Open the folders on a desk or table at the front of the room and have students deliver their papers to the designated folder when they enter class. The first time this happens, chaos will reign, but students will adapt quickly. Organizing papers even into partial alphabetical portions will hasten record keeping.

Folders can be used for the reverse process of handing back papers, but there is a complication that needs to be honored. The Family Educational Rights and Privacy Act (FERPA) that governs a student's right to privacy includes grades. A variety of solutions can be used to follow the law. One option is to put the grade on the Web-based courseware but not on the paper. Another is to write the grade on the back of the assignment, fold it in half, and staple it shut. Some instructors have their students adopt false names or a random arrangement of numbers to honor privacy, though grades should still be concealed.

Technology can ease the paper shuffle tremendously by serving as the conduit for the submission and return of papers and the posting of grades. Passwords keep everything in place, and there are no papers to lose.

Record Keeping

Whether you keep records on the Web or in a notebook of some sort, the only advice is something you already know: Record things in an orderly and timely fashion. You will love yourself for attending to this tedious task as soon as possible. There's no magic here, just a helpful habit to develop.

For many GSIs and faculty, using a computer application is appealing.

Excel and other spreadsheet programs offer the ability to record grades and comments, compiling subtotals and totals as you go. New applications, such as GradeBook, fulfill the basic grading needs and add useful dimensions, for example, updating class lists and other data. Your information technology department will probably have tools for you.

Exercise Versus Display

A key question for an instructor developing an assignment is: Do the structure and the goals of this assignment give students the opportunity to *exercise* or to *display* their learning?

The verbs exercise and display indicate very different types of assignments and different reasons for the assignment. The two overlap, but it is useful to consider these varying aims.

A *display* of knowledge is typically presented in a formal manner. For example, in most presentations the speaker's text is written, visuals of one kind or another are often prepared, and the entire class serves as an audience for the event. The *exercise* of knowledge occurs when students are trying out ideas. This occurs often when, for instance, students talk in class, either in small groups or during whole-class discussions, or when they meet with you and literally practice articulating ideas or forming queries.

Similarly, with writing, we in education are so accustomed to thinking of papers in terms of formal presentations with complete footnotes, clear and concise introductions, revised prose, and so on, that it is hard to break out of the mold. The truth is that a great deal of thinking goes on during informal writing (notes taken while reading or listening, journals, letters, loose jottings about research projects, lists), and we can bring a lot of benefits to our students by validating informal assignments. (Some instructors collect students' notes periodically to see how well they've translated the goings-on in class.) Informal assignments can be graded, too, but instructors should consider the effort and span of exploration as worth more than preliminary findings.

Problem solving also can be part of both formal and informal assignments. Mathematical problems that are required homework but checked randomly by the instructor are an illustration of informal assignments, as is the exercise of having groups of students solve equations during class. For informal assignments, the grading focus shifts away from the tight specifica-

TABLE 9.1
Knowledge: Forms for Display and Forms for Learning

Expressions	Formal	Informal
Writing	Term papers, annotated bibliographies, posters, research papers, essays, Web copy	Class notes, "thinking" papers,* "possible sources" paper,* reaction papers, lists, e-mail
Presentations	Given to whole class, prepared, visual aids	Spontaneous, in small groups, role-playing
Numbers	Prepared, charts and/or graphs, details perfect	Homework exercises or problems, group work

* Described in chapter 10

tions of format and presentation and toward messy accumulation and discovery.

Table 9.1 gives an overview of the variations

A lot of assignments seem automatic—math problems or questions that publishers include at the end of chapters, a short paper in response to an article or a book, and so on. The rhythm of assignments makes good sense in many cases, since the work requires students to pause and use what they have been studying. This rhythm often includes a layering of repetition. Since students carry previously gained knowledge into current assignments, each assignment should help them stretch toward the next learning goal. Sometimes students' energy flags under what they deem repetitious assignments. You may be able to increase motivation with a brief, elegant explanation of the usefulness of repetition.

Motivation

A good deal of research related to students centers on whether students are motivated extrinsically or intrinsically and what the ramifications are of those differing paradigms. I once heard a graduate student discuss research on motivation. She said that motivation increases measurably when people know the reason they're being asked to do something or the purpose that is being served. Such research resonates with common sense. Most of us have been in traffic that stops suddenly for no apparent reason. Curiosity can quickly evolve into impatience. But when we learn the cause—stalled car, a wheelchair whose battery has expired, a stream of baby ducklings flapping after their mother across a highway—patience returns.

Many students are self-motivated to do schoolwork because they want a good grade or they want to learn or they are the kind of people who do what they are told. But even those students will benefit from hearing rationales for assignments, because the rationale often includes connections between the assignment and the bigger issues of the course or discipline or the process they are trying to perfect. For those students who have a hard time focusing on their work, hearing a purpose for the task may be just the nudge they need to get on with it.

One rationale—the biggest probably—for an assignment would be a course goal, such as, "Students will illustrate the actions of cell behavior under stress." This goal contains a process, illustration (pictorial or explanatory), and content. Although you may have gone through the goals at the beginning of the course, most students need to be reminded that assignments are directly linked to those goals. Learning these connections should also help them gain an understanding of the big picture of the course.

Every assignment demands some sort of written, verbal, artistic, or physical expression. Your explanation for practicing the skills can be compelling. If there is an opportunity to show the effects of the assignment being used by people "out in the world" as they landed a desired contract or set up a company or were a finalist for a fellowship, so much the better. Testimonials from guest speakers or former students can be particularly convincing and powerful.

Repetition

It is often easier to recognize the usefulness of repetition in physical development than it is in cognitive development. Obviously practice drills benefit musicians, football players, and swimmers. Students may agree that repetition aids learning geometric equations or verb declensions in a foreign language, but repetition plays an important role in other learning, too.

Long before the explosion that occurred in understanding the science of the brain and how learning happens, William James wrote, "Our nervous systems have . . . grown to the way in which they have been exercised, just as a sheet of paper or a coat, once creased or folded, tends to fall forever afterward into the same identical folds" (as cited in Leamnson, 1999, p. 14). Those of us who watch someone trying to learn something that we know understand this description. Each of us can relate to seeing a string of letters (such as *ayer, ieri, hier,* or *gestern*) that was meaningless until we reached that particular lesson in our foreign language class and *learned* that the letters are words that mean "yesterday"—a word we don't give particular thought to in our native tongue because it is so ingrained.

Repetition gives us these territories of knowledge that grow in complexity and into new connections. Students are at the beginning of many new boundaries and are about to be launched into blazing their own routes of understanding and comprehension.

More recent evidence for the ways that these paths are forged exists in a chapter titled, "How Experts Differ From Novices" in *How People Learn: Brain, Mind, Experience, and School* (Commission on Behavioral and Social Sciences and Education, 2000). Research in disciplines as varied as history and physics illustrate again and again the differences between people who have mastered the discipline (professors in the field for 20 years, for example) and those who are starting out (bright high school students or first-year college students). The results are not about being smart, because the novices are sharp students who know a lot and often apply it well, but the experienced scholars can assess problems more thoroughly and they understand the underlying principles. Thus, they can approach a problem from more than one viewpoint and consider a wider range of solutions.

Repeated exposure to material trains minds into sophisticated thinking—just the kind of thinking we want our students to work toward. The research findings described above illustrate that just as we learn the multiplication tables or the alphabet by repetitious practicing, so do we learn to think by practicing.

Help students extend their practice by not only connecting assignments to course goals but by reminding them that the act of performing the assignment will hone the abilities of their minds. The frequent practice will aid them in constructing the big ideas of your course as well as the big ideas within the discipline. Connecting that knowledge to other disciplines will reinforce their understanding of even bigger pictures—a goal that cannot be achieved without tending to many details, again and again.

Carrots and Sticks—Getting Students to Do Their Homework

In the best of all possible worlds, students would complete their assignments and arrive at class well prepared and ready to fully engage in class. The fact is that students, like all of us, are busy. They have jobs, friends, other courses, and family—all of which demand or want some portion of their time. I believe that most students begin every semester with good intentions to complete assignments, learn the material, and earn a good grade. Distractions and obligations abound.

How do you push your course to the top of a student's priority list? If you establish your course or section as a place where students are engaged with the material, where they are excited about the topics at hand, where they feel respected, where they enjoy contributing and discussing issues with other students and feel a rewarding sense of community, they will want to come to class prepared to participate—the carrot.

Accountability is the most obvious "stick"; it works for all of us—penalties make us feed parking meters, pay our taxes, and set our alarms. If there is a test, if there is a paper due, if there is the expectation of performance, students will make time to work on your course. Tests and papers of many types can call for accountability without being onerous for instructors or for students.

Nurturing a true community where active learning techniques are generously employed can be a powerful incentive for inspiring students to want to arrive in your class well prepared. The stick and the carrot blend well because doing the necessary homework leads to the pleasures and rewards of being part of the class's community. Do not feel bad about giving students assignments whose goals include accountability to the course.

If any students complain about the number of assignments, remind them that keeping up with the work during the term will lighten their study load for finals. I have heard repeatedly about students who wrote on final course evaluations that even though frequent assignments "were sometimes a pain," the accumulation of work made the course easier for them in the long run and they felt they had learned more. We must presume that this learning is exactly what students want to be buying with their tuition dollars.

If you think about the differences between teacher-centered and student-centered classrooms, assignments necessarily take their place as one aspect that reveals sharp contrasts. Historically, the assignments of many disciplines have served as products. "What do you know? Here's your grade." Product assignments will always play an important part in the rhythm of learning and student work.

However, instructors who conduct student-centered courses create assignments that put student learning first. Assignments that emphasize process allow instructors to coach and guide students. As a coach, you can encourage students in their strengths and remind them where the weak spots are and give them some suggestions on how to work on them. By using Vygotsky's (1978) Zone of Proximal Development, as described on p. 17 in chapter 2, you can assess what students know well and what lies at the fringes of their knowledge—the material that they are uncertain about but are *ready* to learn.

This coaching strategy aligns with using informal work of many types, since such assignments often emphasize *process*. Learning occurs during the processes of reading, studying, discussing, drafting ideas, and working on problems. Learning also occurs when students reflect on the material during and following these processes. Assignments can operate as tools that push students to reflect, which is a crucial aspect of comprehension and of improving one's abilities as a learner.

References

Commission on Behavioral and Social Sciences and Education. (2000). *How people learn: Brain, mind, experience, and school.* Washington, DC: The National Academies Press. Retrieved July 20, 2006, from http://www.nap.edu/books/03090 70368/html/

Leamnson, R. N. (1999). *Thinking about teaching and learning: Developing habits of learning with first year college and university students.* Sterling, VA: Stylus.

Vygotsky, L. S. (1978). *Mind and society: The development of higher mental processes.* Cambridge, MA: Harvard University Press.

WHEN STUDENTS WRITE—CONSIDERATIONS AND ASSIGNMENT IDEAS

As one of the two most common expressions in homework or tests, writing is employed by students in the most casual manner when they make notes for themselves. On the other hand, the assignment of a paper can cause anxiety. It is helpful to discuss **Writing—the Emotional Side** with them. Their apprehensions are not uncommon at all.

This chapter offers many **Assignment Ideas** of both a formal and informal nature. An expanded repertoire of assignments not only offers students variety but also allows instructors to select assignments that will be the most effective fit for course material. The ubiquitous term paper serves many learning goals. Examining which assignments are most appropriate for your students may urge you to consider **Term Papers and Their Alternatives** in a new light, not only for specific goals but to help students avoid plagiarism.

Writing—the Emotional Side

Instructors rarely acknowledge to students that there is an emotional component in writing. Written assignments cause many students stress. This is true for first-year students who are assigned a three-page essay, and it is true for PhD candidates as they begin their dissertation. Instructors can help students overcome this alienating sensation by discussing the problem. Any experienced writer will agree that a sense of chaos often reigns during the initial stage while he or she begins to figure out a topic to focus on. As the thesis or the questions to be addressed crystallize, the writer will begin to feel confidence. The task of assembling information can be another phase where writers feel overwhelmed, and then, of course, facing that task of actually writing the draft can also be a time of heightened stress. A cloud of concerns hangs over students: Have I done enough research? Can I write a fabulous, or passable, introduction? Will my arguments be appropriately well-constructed? Can I write a conclusion that makes sense and doesn't sound like a wooden summary?

To imagine that one's emotions can be held in check during these phases is an error, but students (and novice writers) *think* they should feel confident during the whole enterprise. Why not give students the benefit of realizing that apprehensions, fears, and frustrations are common among students at many levels of experiences. Professional writers face the same phases, though repeating the experience helps diminish troublesome emotions. Once writers wend their way through the steps enough times, they become accustomed to the patterns and eventually know, truly, that there will be a satisfactory outcome. Thus patience begins to take the place of anxiety.

If your students are responsible for papers—short or long, exploratory or opinion, research or analytical—tell them about the normality of these emotional reactions. Realizing that anxiety can create roadblocks such as procrastination may bring solace to students and may help them gain control of their work pace.

It is not uncommon during the weeks before a paper is due for instructors to ask students, "How are things coming along?" You might consider passing out file cards for some anonymous responses. Invite them to say if they're overwhelmed or frustrated or haven't begun, for whatever reasons. You can read through these responses very quickly and return to the next class, review some of their comments, and offer some sympathy—and some empathy from your own writing experiences. Offer concrete suggestions, too, of course, including using the services of a librarian or the campus writing center, making an appointment with you, or finding a writing partner.

Assignment Ideas

Daily or weekly assignments fall along a continuum of format and length. Asking students to write down just one question or one quotation from assigned readings may mean that some of them dip into the pages or Web sites long enough to deliver only what's requested. They will do what you ask them to do. If they bring these brief writings to a group, those who are good students or are competitive may devote more effort to the task. As the culture of the class develops into a learning community and students look forward to a session of stimulating intellectual activity, the motivation of the well-engaged students will likely increase, and they will work harder.

It is hard to think about assignments without thinking about grading. In the mind of students and instructors, grading is attached to assignments like barnacles to an old boat. Ease the stress a little bit by using legitimate, fair, and efficient grading methods to assess student work. For many assignments, a simple plus sign, circle, or minus may symbolize Pass/Adequate/Fail or Done/Barely Done/Not Done. Except in the most formal of papers, it is not your responsibility to attend to every spelling error you see. See chapter 13, p. 161, for ideas about grading, particularly the section "Speed Grading," for details.

Assignment Scenarios: Singles, Pairs, Triplets, Quartets, and So On

Here are some skeletal structures that need to be adapted to the content and goals of your course and discipline. Let your imagination play with the possibilities.

- Require students to submit a question, solution, quotation, or point of interest to your class Web site 24 hours before the class.
- Assign students into pairs; require half the class to enter any of the above submissions and require the partner to add a response. Bring the Web site up during class to use the students' paired writings to guide the discussion.
- Use groups of three or four students, and assign roles of producing an argument or solving a problem or responding to one another's questions. Divide the work so that some of it is done on the Web before class and the rest is completed during the session.
- Require a debate among a limited number of students during a live chat Web session (or asynchronously during a set period of time). Those who view it without participating should take the lead during class discussion on the points covered in the debate.

Short Assignments

There are many possible types of short assignments. In some disciplines, it might be appropriate to ask students to come to class with a word of some type, a shape for art, or a portion of a mathematical solution. A sentence offers more possibilities, as might another portion of a problem in math or art, and so does a paragraph. A page or two, or its performance or symbolical equivalent, probably comprises the outer limits of what we might think of as short.

Preparing a good piece of writing that is brief can be a challenging assignment and can serve the purposes of focusing content as well as writing succinctly and clearly. History is replete with examples of powerful pieces of writing that are short. Don't overlook the good work students can achieve by preparing a concise, condensed, summarized, or otherwise short or small assignment.

Low-Tech Alternatives

If you do not use a Web course shareware, you can ask students to e-mail you the assignment, print out their responses, and bring them to class for the same sorts of activities. Or students can simply bring their responses to class where they can be exchanged and discussed.

You can alternate the assignment requests in the list above with other types of responses, including

- single-paragraph or single-page responses to readings or lectures or films or art
- three to five questions on some matter
- an imitation of a problem in the book
- a stanza or quotation from the text
- a summary or review of designated text
- a web of connections from the book—historical events, characters in a book or play, associated people or concepts; students might bring some portion of these and together construct a design that pulls the items into a helpful learning guide.

If you don't want to deal with responses in class, send a group e-mail to the students to summarize your reaction to their work, and use class time for a related discussion that relies on their homework as a platform.

A moderately low-tech assignment would be a creative use of overheads. Give small groups an assignment that needs to be illustrated—a problem to be solved, a flow chart, a hierarchy—and appropriate pens to do their work. After the groups have filled in the overhead, they can give a spontaneous presentation explaining their thinking.

Term Papers and Their Alternatives

Instead of assigning a term paper, consider assigning pieces of that project. A term paper is a product that can be very valuable for students to create, but a great deal of the value comes from steps they must go through along the way. Break the process into smaller assignments. This breakdown not only helps students spend more time on some aspects of research and preparation, but it encourages procrastinating students to keep up.

Following are some ways to break a bigger project into segments. Think of it as a cafeteria and select what suits you, depending upon student learning needs, your time, and your course and discipline.

A Thinking Paper

This task is a low-stress invitation for students to sit down and begin by writing, "What I'm thinking about researching for this project has to do with . . ." The text ought to be first-draft thoughts. Tell students to imagine it as an e-mail to a friend. Assure them that they may run into dead ends as they write, that questions and gaps of knowledge will arise—things to consider pursuing later. Remind them that in this sort of exercise, it is acceptable to stop writing a sentence midway and start another; this is about thinking, not about producing lovely prose, and thinking is messy. Finally—tell them that the writing will not be graded, though the completion of the assignment will. Ask for a full page, because that length will push them into and through initial thoughts and on into unknown territory. This can be a highly valuable exercise.

A thinking paper can stimulate the kind of curiosity and excitement that is required to follow through with the investigation and preparation of a research paper. This investment, too, can put students firmly on the road leading away from plagiarism. If a student turns in a sheet with *nothing* but half sentences, require him or her to come to your office. There you can help the student probe into the topic. There's nothing wrong with helping them develop more clarity in their ideas and then asking them to sit there and write for fifteen minutes.

"Sources I Think I Want to Use"

This activity sends students into the library and to the Internet, or other designated places, looking for possible authors, documents, and sites with appropriate information. The assignment gets them moving, and you will be able to assess the legitimacy and usefulness of their sources. Again this is an assignment that needs no grade. Instead, keep three colors of markers handy, and mark their findings "Great," "Don't use," and "I'm not familiar with this." You shouldn't feel obliged to know every source for every project, but you probably know some key names students should be citing. If you're teaching first-year students, you may recognize some of the trappings of high school researchers—outdated *Time Magazine* articles, general encyclopedia entries, and personal Web sites. Some instructors stipulate the range of sources students should use, for example, "not more than two Web sites, one journal article," and so on, which heads off some possible problems.

Three Initial Paragraphs and a Title

Introductory paragraphs are generally hard to write. Writers, whether students or professionals, can become paralyzed as they play in their mind for the right words to launch a paper. First sentences do not often spring spontaneously.

Thus, an assignment that asks for a few first paragraphs signals to students that you expect students to produce *drafts*, and that what you are looking for are alternative approaches. There are scores of ways to open a paper, and it is a worthy exercise for students to think about that range. Titles, too, signify how topics are approached or dealt with, and they deserve to be tried out. A response to these efforts might be time consuming, since you could indicate in detail what each paragraph implies about the course of the paper, but you could simply assess the writing by putting a 1, 2, or 3 by the paragraphs with brief comments to explain your rating. This assignment is an ideal one for arranging mandatory conferences with students. You might even have students bring the assignment along and read the paragraphs on the spot.

Bibliography

This assignment ranges from the detailed bibliography that is often demanded of dissertation writers to very loosely assembled sources that less-experienced undergraduates might develop. Again, the assignment will force students to delve into their projects and spend enough time with possible sources to get their investigation under way.

You may want to extend this assignment by asking students to put in a sentence or two that describes, "How I think this resource will help me."

Assembly of Findings

Outline? Ordered list? Random compilation?

I have never seen research to substantiate the claim, but in informal conversations on the topic, it seems that, in general, students who are in analytical fields prefer outlines, and those in the humanities don't. This statement is an oversimplification, but you can expect that some of your students will like to create outlines and some will not; for the latter, the idea of an annotated list may be better.

The level of detail in this assignment is up to you. The more that students fill in the topics with sentences containing some content, the more you will be able to see where they are going with the paper and the more work they will have completed or at least drafted for their eventual project.

Rough Draft

This is a big assignment, since it comes right before the real thing. Requiring a rough draft a week or more before the final paper is due cuts down on the number of rough drafts that are turned in *as* final papers—something students admit to doing. Writing a draft can be arduous—it usually is, but the value of the undertaking, if taken seriously, is high; thoughts gain clarity when they are written down. Pushing students through this process, with enough time afterward for them to analyze and revise their work, may help them reflect on all aspects of the project, from their own stewing over the use of a particular word to the strategies, evidence, flow, and construction of the paper as a whole.

Responding to drafts is obviously time consuming, but there are some options. If you are going to review drafts yourself, try to keep focused on the big issues: how the paper develops, whether there is sufficient evidence for claims made, if the research was sufficient, if the introduction and conclusion meet the standards that have been set forth, or other criteria dictated by the assignment. Tell students what you will give most of your attention to so they will not expect a different type of response. (Students may be relieved to know you're not reading the paper with the expectation that it is a finished product.) If a student has a lot of grammar issues, either mark up one paragraph only and explain what you have done, or list some of the problems you see and tell the student to look for them.

A good tool to use for assessing the draft is a rubric or table that allows you to check off boxes that indicate a global reaction to various aspects of the assignment. The rubric on p. 139 is a sample with several conventional aspects of papers that instructors often assess (Figure 10.1). Add or subtract items to suit the goals of your assignment.

A rubric like this one lets you suggest the strengths and weaknesses of the paper without having to write out lengthy details on the copy. You shouldn't hesitate to mark sections that need special attention. You can add asterisks in the rubric to direct students to matching sections. It is always a good teaching practice to give students the rubric ahead of time.

Another method for giving feedback on a draft is to mark one page in detail and tell your students to extrapolate from that page on things they should look for in subsequent pages. You could use this method with the rubric or write additional comments where needed. An important reason not to mark a paper in detail (as tempting as it can be) is to avoid leading students to believe that if they change whatever you mark—because they will assume you have "corrected" *everything* they need to attend to—they will also assume they have fixed all problems and deserve an A. Maybe this will be the case but maybe not. If you don't use a rubric that allows students to see some of the general ways their papers are incomplete, add a brief list of things that need attending to. This addendum will let students know they need to reflect on aspects of the draft and the ways in which they might revise it.

There is no question that going through drafts with any thoroughness requires a great deal of time, but it should make marking the final paper easier. Be sure to ask that the draft be turned in with the final version so you'll have your markings and comments to refer to.

An alternative to such detailed markings—a method that may be necessary depending upon the number of students you have or the frequency of your requiring drafts—is to read some parts with care, skim others, and use

FIGURE 10.1
Sample Rubric for Written Assignment

Aspects of Paper	Needs Work	Adequate	Close to Finished
Thesis is clear and well stated			
Introduction—strong and appropriate			
Transition to body of paper works well			
Good progress in making main points			
Evidence presented well and is valid			
Conclusion pulls claims and evidence together			
Good resources			
Citations and reference list well drafted			
Formatting guide has been followed			
Tone is generally appropriate and consistent			
Grammar and syntax			
Appropriate progress for a draft			
Comments:			

a rubric or checklist to highlight several points. You might even set a timer for five to seven minutes for each paper. Methods like this offer a practical solution to the difficult challenge of wanting to require a draft yet knowing how much time a thorough review will demand.

One last method for managing drafts is with a peer review. Offer your students an appropriate form to use as a response. (This can all be done on the Web, if you don't want to devote class time to it. Be sure to put yourself in the loop to scan the kinds of responses students give one another.) Many checklists include questions with yes/no answers, for example, "Does the writer use appropriate transitions?" Many of these questions are either too general or ask readers for a more sophisticated analysis than most early college students are capable of. Instead, provide prompts that students can respond to with solid answers. A few samples might be

1. What is this paper about?
2. Which part seemed the strongest to you? Why?
3. Describe the place(s) where you felt confused.
4. Did the paper develop in a way that made sense to you? Explain.
5. Did the introduction interest you and set up what followed? Comment.
6. When you reached the conclusion, did you find that it wrapped up preceding material well? Comment.
7. Is there anything else you want to tell the writer?

These kinds of questions invite student readers to engage with the paper as a peer. I've seen students gain immensely from such feedback and alter their work to good effect. The student readers also benefit from scrutinizing another's paper. The process of analyzing someone else's paper helps students examine essay strategies, sentence structures, and even word usage, which helps them do a more thorough revision on their own papers.[1]

Final Paper

A final paper should be a careful revision of the draft presented in the required academic format. When or if you have the opportunity to set your own schedule for assignments, remember to give some thought to having a big paper due several weeks before the end of the course. When students put so much work into a project, it is satisfying for the instructor and the learner to have time to assess how well the work was done before class is over.

Rubrics can again be useful for students working on their paper and for the instructors. You would probably want to add criteria and tighter standards than the rubric on p. 139 demonstrates. A rubric for a final paper should be designed to assess a product rather than a process.

Finally, I would again urge you to consider the purposes of the term paper or its aspects and make use of the portions of the process that serve

---

[1] A good aid to help students write better papers themselves and edit their peers' papers more carefully is a site offered by the University of Chicago to guide first- and second-year students in the humanities and social sciences (Williams & McEnerney, n.d.).

the goals of your course and best aid your students in their learning. Deborah Schoenfelder of the College of Nursing at the University of Iowa uses a few of the assignments above for her unconventional term paper. Her goal for students is that they learn how to think about problems and how to find answers. She assigns students the task of writing an introduction and evaluates it for coherence, but they do not write the entire paper. Every semester some of the students are incredulous about not having to *write* a paper from beginning to end, and they keep checking with her to make sure that it is true. She feels the assignment as she has designed it serves them well for their careers in nursing, because the students focus more time on what she sees as the most important skills for the discipline (D. Schoenfelder, personal communication, October 16, 2006).

Writing a formal research paper is a demanding exercise in thought and self-discipline. These tasks demand the kind of hard work that students need to do as part of their higher education. Nevertheless, creativity can serve you. Depending upon your discipline, you may be able to prescribe a format that is out of the ordinary. For instance, assign a piece for submission to *The Smithsonian*, *Popular Mechanics*, or *Scientific American*. Professional magazines have different tones from academic articles, but their resources are impeccable and the writing is clear and excellent. A white paper prepared for a political body also calls for excellent research and writing but with a unique audience. Length, too, can be altered. Somewhat different skills are needed to develop a good 5-page paper as opposed to a good 20-page paper. Both projects offer learning benefits to the students.

Obviously the range of possible writing assignments is wide. New instructors often develop some of the most inventive assignments because their energy and viewpoints are fresh. Indulge yourself and surprise your students.

Reference

Williams, J. M., & McEnerney, L. (n.d.). *Writing in college, part I*. Retrieved October 9, 2006, from http://writing-program.uchicago.edu/resources/collegewriting/high_school_v _college.htm

II

GROUP WORK AND PRESENTATIONS

Group work has become a frequent tool for teaching and learning. There are sound pedagogical reasons for using groups, but they require planning in order to function well. **Using Groups in Your Classes** introduces the method and raises some considerations, such as how to manage **Gender and Race** or employ groups for **Long-Term Projects**. While groups can provide positive learning experiences, there are ways to **Optimize Group Projects** as well as **Pitfalls to Avoid**. Formal group work is often assessed, at least partly, by presenting material. **Helping Students Give Successful Presentations** offers you ideas to pass along to your students not only to give good presentations in your class but to help them build skills for future courses and postgraduation work.

Using Groups in Your Classes

The first goal of inviting students to begin class by discussing a problem or assignment in groups is to pull their attention into the work of the day. It may be sensible to have the groups work on the same problem or to ask them to address different questions or aspects of their homework. Sometimes group work ends by simply turning to another activity, and sometimes, especially if the groups have worked on different problems, the beneficial conclusion would be to have the whole class hear the results of what each student group discussed.

Having students work in small groups can be highly effective, or it can fall flat. Students who have a strong sense of independence (5% to 10% of the student population, from anecdotes I've heard) may resist and resent being put in groups. Another percentage may have had lousy experiences in groups in previous classes. Good planning on your part with clear assignments and expectations of behavior go a long way toward creating successful group work in your class. Sometimes student learning can be well served with a four- or five-minute jump start into the day, and other times the discussion can be lively and productive for 15 to 20 minutes.

As noted elsewhere, set students up for positive group experiences by giving good guidance:

Poor: "Talk about the article you read for today."
Better: "What was the main idea of the article?"
Best: "Find three pieces of evidence that support the thesis of the article. Pick one of them and discuss its validity."

Whether they are working math problems, discussing the motives of a novel's character, or evaluating one cause of environmental damage versus another, don't let them talk themselves completely out. If you tune into the talk, you can sometimes discern when they've reached their conclusions or hit a stalemate. If the conversation level is still high, given them a one-minute warning, and then pull the class back together to summarize discussions.

The value of group work is greatly enhanced when the groups become teams. According to Larry Michaelsen (Michaelsen, Knight, & Fink, 2002), the elements that guide groups into teams include setting up good procedures to form the groups, accountability measures for the individuals and the groups, excellent assignments, and high-quality responses from the instructor.

When the term starts, have students form groups with those nearby, even though it will result in friends sitting together. The obvious detrimental effect of using proximity as the basis for groups is that friends have lots to talk about besides the course material. More mature friends may work very well together, but groups based on self-selection may not be the most effective. As class continues, use different methods for assembling groups. Random selection (counting off, using students' birth months, and so on) tends to work better overall than the self-selected groups. Groups that are designed by the instructor work the best (Millis, 1999). Faculty and GSIs may select group members because of their participatory behaviors in class or by performance on quizzes or by expressed interests. The criteria may depend heavily on the discipline and the course. A group that can work together effectively is crucial for long-term projects. The project may even be that the group members develop into a team that assembles periodically to discuss assignments.

Barbara Millis (1999), then at the Air Force Academy and teaching a class of 60, switched from a lecture-only format to a more active teaching style. She used groups frequently throughout the semester; she did not know all 60 well, but she watched to see who attended irregularly during the first few weeks so those students could be spread throughout the groups. She wanted to diminish the possibility of forming a group of five that suddenly became a group of two. She noted that the apparent cohesion that developed among group members improved attendance; students came to class much more regularly than they had when she lectured only.

Gender and Race in Small Groups

Some classes have lopsided enrollments. Even if the campus or discipline is fairly even in gender or race, a given discussion section may have a minority of some kind. What to do? Many new instructors assume the best solution is to spread people out—four males in a class, four groups with one male per group. You might be tempted to do the same with the few women or African Americans, Latinos, or international students in your course. Don't try to balance groups. The minority person may either feel no power in the group or feel obliged to try to take it all (I have heard of the latter happening when single males were placed with three or four females). Put yourself in the student's position. If you were in a class with two or three other people who were like you in some way (speak your language, were new to America, were your gender), you might appreciate having a peer in your small group, at least initially, rather than feeling artificially placed in separate groups. Additionally, students can see what's going on, and it feels embarrassing to everyone. Avoid the situation by watching students select their own groups for a while. Within a few classes, as students become better acquainted, they may organize themselves differently, or you will see those who are more comfortable and ready to be aligned along other criteria.

Long-Term Projects

I worked with an instructor who taught a course on museum exhibits. Students created a list of possible projects and he honed them by using a method of multiple votes. The students ended up in groups according to their interest—an ideal method for motivating students during a term's worth of research, tasks, and activities.

Long-term assignments obviously need to be demanding and multi-stepped. They should be too complex for even a good student to fulfill in the allotted time frame. A good analogy is the production of a play. The people doing scenery are not going to have any substantive time to worry about costumes, though they may want to have a few discussions with the person doing the lighting. Actors, meanwhile, are not going to occupy themselves with those in charge of promotion.

Group projects can provide an opportunity for a lot of creativity. Making a movie, preparing an exhibit, building a Ferris wheel, or planning a fund-raiser may be outside the realm of your discipline's customary scholarly activities, but you can imagine that students could learn a great deal by approaching a topic from an unusual direction. (Remember, students' final products can convey a great deal of work and learning without including the actual final product.) If you can push an assignment into an unconventional form, you may find that student energy and engagement are surprisingly high.

Optimizing Group Activities

Like most assignments, clear expectations provide the best foundation for group projects—large or small. Specified roles can also facilitate successful group work. Roles that instructors can offer to students, whether singly, by pairs, or as a group, include

- library research
- online research
- problem-solving work
- interviews
- writing and its phases
- materials assembly
- presentation preparation—posters, structures, experiments, media
- other activities devised by you or by the students.

Anthony R. Brunello, professor of political science at Eckerd College in Florida, credits his successful career to the wisdom and mentoring he received under James C. Davies at the University of Oregon, who believed that "students learn best when allowed to help teach each other" (A. R. Brunello, personal communication, August 8, 2006). Brunello adds that group work offers the opportunity to place a "high emphasis on leadership responsibility." He says that instructors should use this opportunity to interview students who want to be a group's leader rather than selecting one simply because the student volunteers.

As students plan their projects and sign up for tasks, they should develop a timeline to mark progress. In some disciplines—engineering, for example—timelines are an integral part of any project.

Other tools that help groups function well are checklists. You might ask for a weekly report, which will help students stay on task. To help focus the summary, list a few questions for students to answer, such as:

- In which ways is your group operating well?
- Are there frustrating aspects to the group's project?
- Who would you consider to be the best contributor to the project?
- What do you hope to accomplish in the coming week?

Reports might be prepared by the leader, the whole group, or by alternating members. Group work is always an experiment, like much of teaching, so instructors should feel free to try one method and then another.

Another sort of report is an evaluation sheet, where students grade their peers. A common design gives each group member one hundred points to assign among his or her peers. Figure 11.1 on page 148 shows an example.

An added option would be to provide space for students to give reasons for the point distribution.

Some teachers completely abdicate responsibility for groups that fail together. The attitude there is that the students are responsible for making their peers do the work. I'm not sure what that really achieves educationally. Responsible students will make sure the work is completed, and instead of feeling a rich pride about their achievement, the students will more likely carry frustrations about the slacker(s) and resentment toward you for ignoring their troubled process.

Pitfalls of Group Projects

One of the biggest reasons students resist group projects is because of slackers—people who do not do their share of the work. Slackers are particularly dreaded when the group is assigned a single grade.

FIGURE 11.1
Sample Group Self-Evaluation Form

Assign points to your group peers with the following criteria in mind: • attended meetings promptly and reliably • offered helpful ideas • followed through on individual assignments • gave support and help to others	
	Points Assigned
Jill	
Simon	
Maury	
Mina	
Torin	

Total Points   100

As students know, the goals of course projects include not only mastering and presenting content but also coordinating tasks in order to bring all the pieces of the assignment together in good time. In order to keep the problem of irresponsible members from becoming an overblown and distracting issue, offer students two options.

Allow groups to fire a slacker. Reasons may include not communicating, not coming to meetings, not fulfilling agreed-upon tasks by deadline, or otherwise being a pain in the neck (students will laugh, and they will know precisely what you mean). In order to effect the firing, the group must compose a letter to you detailing the problems and making the request. Brunello, who has done extensive research in small-group success, says, "Sometimes, the result of the 'intent to fire' produces these wonderful opportunities for forgiveness and redemption." He says that people ask for a second chance "and often they make good on their opportunity" (A. R. Brunello, personal communication, August 8, 2006).

The flip side of this idea is to allow students to resign from their groups. The same sorts of reasons can supply the cause, and again a letter must be written to you to make the request.

These options inform everyone that you know how groups can go wrong and that you care about the group functioning well. From anecdotal evidence, this structure inspires more individual responsibility among members and helps keep the focus on the project.

Helping Students Give Successful Presentations

It has become rather common to require presentations as part of a larger assignment. Give students some of the same public speaking tips that have been offered to instructors in this book. They have probably heard lots of them before, but hearing the tips from you will let them know what your standards are. The strategies employed by actors are not to be ignored, even though the actions can feel awkward to people who don't see themselves in that artificial role.

Fundamental suggestions for a successful presentation are to speak at an appropriate pace, speak loudly enough, take care not to let jargon trip out too fast, and not to drop the voice at the end of sentences. Students *ought* to go to a large room and practice. Or you might guide them through a dry run prior to their presentation, which is similar to what I've done in my course on teaching and learning in higher education. I invite the students (new faculty and GSIs) to stand in a circle and deliver the first few sentences of the introduction to their course as if they were at an initial class meeting—everyone speaks at once. People laugh, of course, because it's cacophonous. Then I ask them to do it a second time—louder, clearer, and more slowly. Even in the chaos of voices, the rhythms and clarity noticeably improve. And the point is made. They understand that they *can* improve what they think they already know how to do.[1] Students should also be urged to practice in front of roommates or have themselves filmed by friends.

You also might remind your students that this is practice—as are many activities in college—for whatever they do after college. It is impossible to overemphasize the many uses and importance of public speaking skills for their future careers. Any student can imagine the extreme embarrassment of being the newest employee on the block who is invited to make a few remarks at a meeting and finds himself being interrupted by a senior employee down the table with a request to speak up.

---

[1] My thanks to Nancy Houfek, head of voice and speech for the American Repertory Theatre and Institute for Advanced Theatre Training at Harvard University, for this public speaking exercise, who conducted a workshop on this topic some years ago that I had the good fortune to attend.

Regarding the methods of shaping content for public presentation, the old saw about telling people what you're going to tell them, then telling them, and then telling them what you have told them is only a slight exaggeration of fairly solid advice. In many cases it is precisely the best recipe, though this should not mean that the first, middle, and final paragraphs are identical. Any talk that sounds as if it's fulfilling a prescribed formula will sound artificial to the audience. The introduction should give a broad picture of what is to follow, the specifics should be clarified appropriately, perhaps with visual aids, and the conclusion should tie things together. Audiences appreciate a good conclusion that reassures them that they have made proper sense of a talk.

Visual aids? To PowerPoint or not to PowerPoint. Most students have become highly skilled in developing PowerPoint slides, because it has become a common activity in schools across the country from the early grades on. Slides, in addition to providing headings or lists, may include film clips, shots of historical documents, and animations to illustrate an aspect of the students' research. Visual aids can add a great deal to a talk, but they can also deflect attention from the speaker. Even if the visual product makes up most of the project, it is of key importance that the presenter perform the crucial task of guiding the audience through the content. If you have more than one presentation in a term, I would invite you to consider assigning one presentation without prepared visual aids. The constraint means there is more pressure on students to perform well as speakers, which is good practice for them.

In a graduate course I taught, I assigned a presentation about a historical aspect of education from a selected list of books. I said nothing about PowerPoint or any other visual aid. Two of the highly experienced GSIs chose to use PowerPoint. I was struck by how PowerPoint influenced the amount of eye contact they gave to the class, which was extremely diminished. Both presentations had interesting content and both presenters had excellent presentation skills, but as their eyes spent more and more time on the screen, I noticed the audience of students, who were all seriously interested in the course, glancing around, sliding in their chairs a bit, and slowly slipping in their attention.

Later, my research assistant, Suzanne Swiderski, looked for information on the topic of eye contact in the classroom. There was not much to be found, though Mayer (2005) found evidence that students learned better when they received a lot of eye contact from their teachers. Nothing was found in regard to PowerPoint slides. I hope some enterprising researcher will undertake a study about this phenomenon vis-à-vis PowerPoint and other such teaching tools. In the ongoing effort to improve the effectiveness of teaching, especially teaching with technology, research findings would help us refine our methods. In the meantime, if your students plan to use visual aids, remind them to make a special effort to look at students, even while students are glancing from the presenter to the slides and back. If speakers have a hard copy of the slides near them, they may be less inclined to look unnecessarily at the screen.

Good presentation skills are difficult to develop because opportunities to practice do not arise often, compared to, say, opportunities to write. Discussions in class provide many chances for informal speaking, but graded presentations raise the tension by specifying the length of a talk and various other formal aspects. Despite how nerve-racking students may find the assignment, they will derive much from the practice. Remind them that it is one more benefit of their tuition.

References

Mayer, K. (2005, October). Fundamentals of surgical research course: Research presentations. *PubMed.* Retrieved October 1, 2006, from http://www.ncbi.nlm.nih .gov/entrez/query.fcgi ? cmd = Retrieve&db = pubmed&dopt = Abstract&list _uids = 16243041&query_hl = 2

Michaelsen, L., Knight, A., & Fink, D. (2002). *Team-based learning: A transformative use of small groups.* Westport, CT: Praeger.

Millis, B., & Cottell, P. (1999). *Using groups both wisely and well. Basic structure and management tips. Q & A session.* Lake Harmony, PA: Professional Organization Development Network in Higher Education, annual meeting.

12

FRAUD, CHEATING, PLAGIARISM, AND SOME ASSIGNMENTS THAT DISCOURAGE IT

How wonderful it would be to omit a chapter on these topics in a book about teaching, but unfortunately the topic is one that must be given quite a bit of attention. Unethical actions to achieve better grades have spawned broad concerns about **Fraud in Higher Education. Cheating**, for instance, has probably been around as long as tests have, but new technology has inspired new ways of doing it. Technology has also become a tool for people to use to avoid some types of assignments, particularly writing papers. Faculty members and GSIs can help students work toward reaching the goals of a course by giving some thought to **Plagiarism and Assignments That Discourage It**. Well-constructed assignments can go a long way toward eliminating the onerous and time-consuming work of **Dealing With Students Who Cheat or Plagiarize**.

Fraud in Higher Education

Unfortunately, cheating of various types has undeniably been on the rise in recent decades, fueled by a number of things, including high-stakes courses, competition for graduate school slots, computer and Web capabilities, and other technological innovations in cell phones, iPod expansions, and so on.

When you introduce the discussion of cheating, plagiarism, and fraud to your class, you might begin by saying, as I said above, that you wish you didn't need to raise the issue, but that you must because of the following:

1. Rise in cheating[1]
2. Rise in plagiarized papers
3. Theft of exams
4. Departmental policy
5. University policy
6. Fraudulently won grades

By merely raising the issue, you let students know that you are paying attention to the problem, and they may be less likely to chance it in your class. If you think your students would like an economic comparison, you might ask them how they would feel about buying a computer that contains only half the software offered or booking a flight whose pilot knows how to manage only part of the plane's controls. Why would students (and their parents) spend the many thousands of dollars required these days for a college education and deprive themselves of learning everything they possibly can in this final (for most of them) phase of their formal education? In addition, future employers as well as parents and alumni expect that graduates will possess the skills that their degrees represent.

The truth is that when students reach college, there *ought* to be a change in the attitude that teachers (professors, GSIs, tutors) are there to drag students through courses, readings, homework assignments, and listen to the question, "Will this be on the test?" The attitude should shift to students embracing the opportunities before them, taking responsibility for managing their learning and grappling with confusion, and gaining an understanding that one of the largest differences between college and their previous educational experiences is that when they graduate, they enter a world where people everywhere will make fresh assumptions about them.

To the world, having a college education means having read and analyzed a range of works, learned about various aspects of history and philosophy, and tackled theories in a range of areas. This expectation is true for students coming from Omaha or Orlando, New York City or San Diego. Students will enter a club with common denominators, common expectations about what they have studied, how they've studied, and how to continue learning. No matter where they land a job, if they are working with

---

[1] Find out if there has been a local scandal in recent years, and describe it; *The Chronicle of Higher Education* has published over a dozen articles annually during the past three years about some aspect of academic fraud.

other college graduates, topics will arise that they have all studied and thought about.

Cheating

If students cheat on tests and skip the hard work of researching and writing papers by purchasing prepared papers or copying great chunks from the Internet or obtaining answers to homework assignments by illegitimate means, they are indeed cheating themselves and their futures. They are also degrading the institution, an institution held dear by most of the previous students who believe a degree from Hardwork University represents a valuable achievement. The idea of fairness is nearly as American as apple pie, and focusing on that virtue may be the most powerful antidote against cheating.

David Callahan, author of *The Cheating Culture: Why More Americans Are Doing Wrong to Get Ahead,* writes that "some surveys [find] that up to three-quarters of college students cheat" (2006). Callahan believes that students rationalize their own cheating because they see so many public figures cheat to achieve success. He says that "to cast the issue as a matter of justice" is the most likely way to dissuade students from the practice.

You might think that a mini-lecture covering these issues would turn the most disenchanted student into a scholar eager to do all the hard work of scholarship, but it probably doesn't work on everyone. Thus, your institution supplies a range of censures and penalties.

When you discuss plagiarism or cheating with your class, explain the campus policies and consequences. In some schools, cheating on a test or plagiarizing a paper will lead to an F for that event and that event alone. A letter may go into a student's files, but he or she can pass the course and graduate unscathed. In other places, at the University of North Dakota, for instance, a student caught cheating is booted out of school. It is a zero-tolerance school.

One benefit of giving the talk about these behaviors is that it helps reassure those who don't cheat that they will be less likely to suffer from a skewed curve, and it also lets everyone know that you'll be attentive during exams. It is common sense for instructors to implement several rules for test day, especially for large or cramped classes; these policies may include restrictions on cell phones and other electronics, a prohibition against hats or hoods, and so on. One of the most recognized ways to deter cheating is to proctor, so despite the temptation to read or grade papers, walk around the room frequently. Your department or professor may have additional ideas, and you can find tips on several Web sites of faculty development centers.[2]

Plagiarism and Assignments That Discourage It

Concerns about plagiarized papers in college used to be connected to a filing cabinet at the fraternity house. Those days seem nearly quaint in light of how widespread the problem has become. Students learn how to use computer programs and the Internet at an early age. Many report that they were not corrected in high school when they copied text from a Web site into a paper without citing the source. No wonder some of them come to college feeling puzzled about the fuss surrounding plagiarism.

An assignment such as, "Write a 15-page paper on Dante's *Inferno*" or "Write a 10-page paper on the financial failures of the Stock Market in 1987" is unfortunately an invitation, especially for students who are short of time, to go to the Web where papers that suit the requirement can be purchased for $40 to $70 on sites such as Schoolsucks and Termpapers. Sadly, these sites even offer papers on demand, written by freelancers to fulfill a specific assignment.

In some courses, instructors locate a free student paper from their discipline on the Web and ask their students to read it and critique it as a small-group activity in class or as a threaded discussion on a class Web site. This exercise lets students know that you're aware of what is available, and it gives them a chance to be thoughtful about the actual quality of the free papers.

Instructors can lessen the temptations of students to commit fraud by avoiding traditional assignments. The two chief methods of doing so are to use the activities and conversations in your own class as a basis for assignments or to use novel assignment structures.

The first type depends upon stretching the assignment to two or more phases. Link activities and discussions from the classroom to small tasks that may, if it suits you, become part of larger assignments. An example of ways to break down the writing of a term paper can be found on pp. 135–141 in chapter 10.

Another technique to employ is that of *scaffolding*, a term connected to

---

[2] See, for example, "Tips to Prevent Cheating" from the University of California at Davis at http://trc.ucdavis.edu/trc/services/testing/cheat.html

Lev Vygotsky's (1978) Zone of Proximal Development, described in chapter 2. Scaffolding requires the instructor to guide a student to what the student is learning, "engage students' interest, simplify tasks so they are manageable, and motivate students to pursue the instructional goal" (Riddle & Dabbagh, 1999). Essentially, the teacher needs to mediate between the student and the task to keep the student attached to and believing in the project. With such involvement from both sides, the likelihood of plagiarism decreases dramatically.

Here are a few additional ideas.

Assign teams to interview each other on course readings or assignments and prepare an appropriate summary.

Use pairs to "pass the baton." Create an assignment with two parts. Have one student complete part one, then have the student pass it to his or her partner, who must rely on what the first student did, to complete part two. You might also have the students switch roles for another pair of activities. The pieces can, of course, be modified according to the goals of different assignments and to a variety of media.

Some methods for creating alternative assignments would be to

- Ask students to interview a local person regarding actions or policies relevant to your course content.
- Ask students to write a dialogue between two people they have been studying.
- Ask students to create a list of paragraphs, quotes, or sample problems from sources you give them or sources you tell them to locate. Such a task resembles an annotated bibliography, but instead of the typical forms of annotation, students will locate a piquant or cogent paragraph, explanation, diagram, problem set, or comment type that you designate. As with a typical bibliography assignment, they should include all citation information.
- Ask students to employ their knowledge about a media form to analyze material. They might create a portion of "director's notes" for the destruction of an overpass, a re-creation of a historical event, or the announcement of a merger.
- Use the form of a letter or a memo with invented roles for students and the audience the memo is addressed to.

- Invite students to adopt the voice or style of a newscaster to report on and then analyze an event in your discipline.

Another direction to take, which overlaps with the suggestions above, involves asking students to discuss points made by other students during a discussion in person or online.

Another source of assignments is your department. Compare assignment ideas with your peers. Lots of suggestions float around that can be modified for your purposes. The more inventive you are, the less likely that students will fulfill the assignment in a fraudulent manner. A final reason—not to be overlooked—for developing an assignment in an unusual way is that students may attend to a creative assignment partly because they will be excited by the novelty of the design. They are accustomed to the kinds of class activities that are so familiar to all of us. A fresh way of approaching a problem can be captivating and intriguing.

Dealing With Students Who Cheat or Plagiarize

Your department or institution undoubtedly has a detailed plan about who to contact and how to go about handling a student you suspect of cheating or plagiarizing. Below are a few general ideas to consider.

Google has helped many GSIs and faculty members determine that a student used text from the Internet. When you enter a unique string of five or six words with quotation marks around the phrase, you will see a list of sites that include the language. A more thorough searching source is the Turnitin Web site. If your institution subscribes to this service, you can go to the appropriate Web page, submit an electronic version of a student's paper, and in a short time, you'll receive a report on the percent of the paper that is repeated from other sources, plus a list of those sources. You can scroll through the paper to see which sections are duplicated and from which sources. This service is a boon for determining if a paper has been plagiarized. (Some institutions make this site available for students, so they can check their work before turning it in, and some instructors require that they do so.)

Regardless of which method you use, print out the page(s) with the relevant text, and ask your student to come to see you. If you're a GSI, tell your teaching supervisor what has happened and ask if he or she wants to sit in on the meeting.

When the student arrives, tell him or her that there is a problem with the paper, and show the student the comparisons. (Use the same strategy if two students turn in the same or virtually the same paper or examination.) Ask the student why this duplication might have happened. Then, the best thing to do might be to remain quiet and let the student digest the situation. I have heard of three scenarios occurring at this point: (a) The student will confess and begin making explanations, (b) the student will deny there is a problem and generally within a short time accept the blame, or (c) the student will claim he or she has written papers like that for years and be completely surprised that you think this is a problem.

You may want to have handy a copy of the institutional protocol for the consequences of plagiarizing, which might include assigning an F to the paper, assigning an F to the course, allowing the student to rewrite the paper, or whatever else your institution calls for. Whether a student will weep, rage, or slink out of the office depends upon that student. Keep the office door open, and make sure someone in the area knows what is taking place.

A very important aspect about this sort of event relates to keeping meticulous records about what and when and who. Print relevant e-mails, make notes about conversations and so forth, and compile all documentation relating to the plagiarism and the meeting. Regardless of how strict or lenient your institution's stand on plagiarism, you may well be required to write a letter to your chair and possibly a dean about the allegations and evidence.

Cheating on a test is a slightly different situation, since students are often caught during the examination itself. If, despite all the precautions you take, you see students copying from cheat aids or from other students, observe for a short while to be certain that cheating is indeed under way. To avoid disrupting the whole class, hand the student a copy of the college's policy on cheating while you take the student's paper away. Check with your teaching supervisor about this method, but it seems to be much cleaner than waiting until after the test and raising accusations that could turn into a type of "he said/she said" argument.

This policing aspect of college instruction is anathema to those of us who seek teaching as a vocation. As in many situations in life, the best offense is a good defense. Do everything you can to discourage fraudulent schoolwork in the first place to lessen the possibility of problems occurring later.

References

Callahan, D. (2006, May 8). A better way to prevent student cheating. *Christian Science Monitor.* Retrieved October 11, 2006, from http://www.csmonitor.com/2006/0508/p09s02-coop.html

Riddle, E. M., & Dabbagh, N. (1999). *Lev Vygotsky's social development theory.* Retrieved December 3, 2007, from http://www.balancedreading.com/vygotsky.html

Vygotsky, L. S. (1978). *Mind and society: The development of higher mental processes.* Cambridge, MA: Harvard University Press.

13

GRADING

Concerns with grading begin with **Institutional Requirements**. In the classroom, faculty and GSIs need to consider **Two Mandates in Grading** that pertain to instructional ethics. **Learning Outcomes** are an aid for students and teachers. **Rubrics**, too, though developed as a tool for grading, can be a powerful aid to students as they work on assignments. Ideas for **Test Construction** will help you create questions for multiple-choice, essay, and short-answer examinations.

Beyond the practical and mechanical aspects of grading lie some overarching issues that may influence the work of GSIs but need particular attention from new faculty. Among these are **Improvement as a Factor**, **Nonnative English Speakers**, **Weighting Grades**, **Gatekeeping Knowledge**, and **Extra Credit**.

If you are **Grading Attendance**, one challenge is grading **Engaged Participation**, an aspect of which is **Keeping Track of Participation**. Depending upon the assignments you oversee, you may be in charge of **Assessing Public Speaking** or **Grading Group Presentations**.

Regardless of how great or limited your responsibilities are for a course, you will find useful tips among the suggestions in **Efficient Grading: Blocking Time and Space, Staggered Due Dates, Speed Grading, Brief and Frequent Assignments, Assessing Grammar, Surprise Postponement, Marginalia or Endnotes**, and **Making Use of Technology, Templates, and Timers**.

Finally, the possibility of **Grade Complaints** must be addressed. Most courses end with **Student Evaluations of You**.

G rades are an inescapable aspect of teaching—one that many new faculty members and GSIs find distasteful, since judgment sits in direct opposition to the coaching and mentoring relationship that instructors often develop with students. The challenge can be especially difficult for GSIs who are close in age to students and who run sections or work in drop-in help centers where the tasks are more like tutoring than full instruction. While the term *grading* will remain an inescapable part of education, thinking about the full process of assessment may be more productive.

The idea of assessment overlaps with the idea of grades, but grades are attached to aspects of performance—assignments, problem sets, tests—while assessment may be a measurement instrument (examination) or an umbrella concept. If we think of how assessment works in other fields, such as medicine, environmental studies, or library collection management, we imagine that salient attributes are being examined for their robustness, their privations, their changes in growth or development, the directions they seem to be heading, and so on. An instructor of a class of 20 to 30 gathers a lot of information about students by observing attendance, participation, and quality of homework or assignments. One hopes that a grade assigned to an examination is an overall reflection of all of the students' actions, but that may not necessarily be the case. If a test doesn't measure what you know about a student's engagement and apparent learning, invite him or her to come to your office and discuss ways the student might alter study strategies or test preparation. Test anxiety takes a toll on some students.

College instructors are responsible for grading students, not assessing them, but instruction that places student learning in the center of the course includes attention to student progress as well as student accomplishment. Discovering what and how well students are learning can also influence an instructor's methods and pace of teaching. Seen in this light, grading has student learning at its center (Walvoord & Johnson Anderson, 1998).

Departments may prescribe the assessment instruments for some courses, especially in lower-division courses in large colleges where hundreds of students are enrolled in many sections. However, new faculty and some new GSIs may immediately carry responsibilities for grading.

Given that, the sections below cover areas of consideration, whether and how to grade attendance and participation, tips for grading efficiently, and so on. The goal of the chapter is to attend to the whole matter of assessing students, not exhaustively but through offering suggested threads that you will develop as your career evolves.

Depending upon your appointment and discipline, some aspects of the grading processes and options may not be of specific concern to GSIs, but familiarity with this material will give you an overview of current practices and help you consider your own evaluation methods in the future.

Institutional Requirements

Among the top tier of stringent if not rigid institutional requirements are those surrounding grades. There is generally little leeway for violating these policies. Depending upon your school you will be expected to comply with departmental guidelines, submit grades on schedule, follow protocols for suspected cheating or plagiarism, and send appropriate notifications to sports personnel or your department for specified students.

Two Mandates in Grading

The cardinal rule of grading is that a test must be aligned with assigned material. This point may seem obvious, but in fact it doesn't always occur. In the same way that a course has designated goals and that assignments are connected to those goals, an examination, too, should link to the goals through the course work and activities. Students should not be surprised by tests.

Students should also not be surprised by the grading method that is used. If students believe they will be given multiple-choice tests and that their letter grade will depend upon the number of correct questions, they will be very dismayed to learn, for instance, that all of the students' grades will be placed on a curve and letters assigned according to the range.

Grading methods must be transparent from the beginning. If you decide spontaneously to toss out a grade because everyone does poorly, you probably won't hear complaints, but if, once the syllabus has been distributed, you embrace a revised grading scheme that even hints at conceivably unfair or surprise grading practices, the havoc may be large and long lasting. Grading plans are one of the few things that must be set in stone from the beginning.

Learning Outcomes

"Learning outcomes are statements of what is expected that a student will be able to DO as a result of a learning activity" (Jenkins & Unwin, 1996, paragraph 2). Some colleges want instructors to write learning outcomes for their courses so that expectations of what students will gain can be transparent to the department and to accrediting agencies. If you prefer to think in terms of graphics, course-level outcomes fall under the larger outcomes for majors, which are linked to those of a program, and then the department. When learning outcomes are available to the public, via Web sites perhaps, students know precisely what, with enough work, they can expect to achieve in the class.

Learning outcomes need to be specific, and they need to focus on behaviors, skills, accomplishments, or abilities that can be measured. In preparing outcomes, use active verbs, such as "demonstrates," "illustrates," "performs," rather than verbs that cannot be made visible, such as "knows," "learns," or "understands." Lists of verbs related to the cognitive levels of Bloom's Taxonomy are listed on p. 19 in chapter 2 and would be good tools to use for composing learning outcomes.

The guidelines in the section on writing course goals offers a model similar to what is expected for learning outcomes. For instance, a course goal may be: "This course will help students understand the differences between personal and persuasive essays." A learning outcome based on that goal may be: "Students will draft, edit, proofread, and polish two personal essays and two persuasive essays and discuss the attributes that distinguish each type."

The point is that both the *actions* and *products* described in learning outcomes can be assessed.

Rubrics

A rubric is a grading guide created for a specific assignment or examination. The rubric offers a breakdown of the way attributes of an assignment fulfill the criteria of an A, B, and so on. Rubrics can be developed and used advantageously for assignments, presentations, performances, and essay exams. An extra activity in class would be to have students work in groups to develop a rubric for a meal, a film, or an apartment. The exercise makes the point of the challenge of assessing quality. Students also realize that two dissimilar expressions in one attribute can both signify equal quality. The guides are designed in many formats including lists, paragraphs, grids, and charts. Their common structure is to describe various attributes of an individual assignment according to several levels of quality. For instance, a rubric for a speech would include "clarity of speaking." Examples of low-, mid-, and high-qualitative descriptors might read in the following way: "mumbles, slurs," "occasional swallowed words," and "crisply spoken with good expression and pacing."

Specificity in a rubric is very important. A vague guideline such as, "Introduction is clear" does not offer much guidance. Instead, a standard description such as, "Introduction engages reader and sets forth appropriate tone and direction of essay" or "states goal of paper" or "describes foundation and authority of thesis" gives the grader and student a much clearer understanding of how to assess or achieve high quality.

One of the most important uses of a rubric is as a guide for students. Students have a vague idea of what a quality assignment should look like, but why shouldn't they see a specific layout of the important attributes and the ways to fulfill the assignment? Include a copy of your guide—hard copy or on the Web—when you give the assignment.

When a group of GSIs grade the same assignment, a rubric of some sort—designed by the group or the professor—can be extremely helpful for achieving standardization. A good rubric not only helps you grade well and efficiently, it also helps you communicate to students the standards and expectations of the assignment.

The sample rubric in Figure 13.1 might be for a proposal for a paper in, say, sociology, archaeology, or urban studies. It is designed to measure an assignment with specific guidelines about what should be included and how the information should be conveyed and substantiated. You may notice that it includes nothing about logic, tone, creativity, or many attributes that may be important in other assignments.

This rubric contains a specific number of types of evidence. Although it has a mechanical feel, if the assignment needs a specific number of something in order to earn a particular grade, then the number should be in the rubric.

Each box in the rubric lists more than one attribute. As the instructor, you can decide if you want to cross lines. For instance, if a paper contains five pieces of evidence but the explanations respond to criteria under 2 or 3, the paper doesn't deserve the best mark.

Another rubric option is to open boxes. For instance, the contents under Central Argument and Accuracy of Details could be one category. The more categories you have, the more different ways you will need to assess the paper, which often means spending more time with it. An important aspect,

FIGURE 13.1
Sample Rubric

Score	1	2	3	4
Proposition or Introduction	Proposition is specific and concise	Proposition is general, though clear	Proposition states case, but includes side issues	Proposition has excessive side issues or is unclear
Central Argument	Five types of evidence, well-explained, connections are smooth and strong	Four types of evidence, explanation is adequate, connections are apparent	Three types of evidence, explanations are thin but comprehensible, few connections	Two types of evidence, explanations are scanty, no connections
Accuracy of Details	Support is generous and specific, many well-cited facts and sources	Support is broad and mostly specific, some facts and sources	Support is general, few facts or sources	Support is vague, one or two facts or sources
Means of Communication	Sentence structure and word choice vary, figures and tables are clear and sufficient	Sentences and word choice are clear, figures and tables make sense	Sentences and word choice are generally clear, most figures and tables make sense	Sentences are poorly structured and word choices confusing, figures and tables are incomplete
Appearance and Format	*APA* guidelines for font, page and table lay-out, citations, and numbers are followed	Most *APA* guidelines are followed	Some *APA* guidelines are followed	Few *APA* guidelines are followed

though, is that once you score, say, a half dozen papers with a rubric, your familiarity with its features will accelerate your grading.

Test Construction

Constructing exams is a challenging task. Obviously it takes longer to build a multiple-choice test than an essay exam, but the former is faster to grade. Many textbooks offer banks of multiple-choice questions with an accompanying disk or an online service. In some disciplines, this format is the only kind of test used; in others, it is never used. Essay exams are faster to create yet take longer to grade. Other options, such as short-answer tests, fill in the blanks, and matching items in one list to items in another list fill a middle ground of time to create and time to grade. GSIs may not have any control over test construction, or they may have quite a bit. I knew a professor of a large class whose GSIs were responsible for turning in two questions after each of the weekly lectures. The professor selected the best ones to create the periodic exams.

Exams where GSIs or faculty members give out the questions early are obviously very beneficial for student learning. Give students six essay questions and tell them that two of them will make up the test. This plan allows them to study and practice writing about the big issues of the class. It also removes the mystery of what will be on the test. Even if you're using a multiple-choice format, you can give out "big questions" as a study guide that will allow students to focus their studying from a different viewpoint than simply reviewing their notes.

If you have the responsibility for creating a test, return to the course goals and the learning outcomes. As noted earlier in the chapter, the outcomes need to be represented by activities and products that can be assessed. Consider a specific session with your students, a reading, or another assignment, and think about the ways each connects to the actions and tasks in your outcomes. Questions that are tightly linked to outcomes are exemplary samples of the practice of testing the content of a course. GSIs and faculty members sometimes develop questions as the term goes along, thereby creating their own bank of items to draw from for short or long tests.

Once you've noted relevant material, decide how you want to test the material—essays, short answer (essays of a paragraph or so), multiple-choice or true-or-false questions, or matching, fill in the blank, and so on. Below are samples and tips for writing effective tests. Many of the tips are true for all test construction, including using appropriate language, letting questions sit for a few days so you can double-check them for clarity and purpose, avoiding anything tricky, and so on.

When you've settled on a format, turn to the cognitive levels from Bloom's Taxonomy as described on p. 19 in chapter 2. Select as many levels as suit the exam and choose verbs to anchor your questions.

The following are two samples of cognition levels with sample questions that fit the categories:

Physics Example

Memorization: What is chaos theory?

Illustration: Describe chaos theory as it operates in turbulent fluids.

Explanation: Using chaos theory, explain the connection between weather and climate.

Analysis: Why do Julia sets exist between Fatou sets? Use hurricanes to help explain your answer.

Literature Example

Memorization: Who were the main characters (list at least 10) in *Pride and Prejudice*, and how are they related to one another?

Illustration: Give three examples of conflict in the B family.

Explanation: Explain Mrs. B's interest in Mr. C.

Analysis: Why did Mr. D go to London to confront Mr. W? Be thorough.

This second set shows a pitfall of test construction—hinting at or giving away the answer to one question with information in another. This challenge can be a stickler. In this instance, one creative solution would be to put the first question on its own piece of paper. Have students bring their answer to you when they are through, and then give them the rest of the test.

When writing essay questions, be sure to give yourself time to put the question away for a while so you can edit it well before giving it to students. Sometimes questions turn into lengthy essays of their own. I recall a GSI complaining about the inadequacy of responses to an essay assignment she'd given students. When she showed it to me, the students' problem was immediately obvious. The assignment consisted of three long, single-spaced paragraphs that filled most of a page. There were too many qualifiers, conditions, and considerations. It would have taken a student a very long time to determine precisely what the instructor was looking for. Be succinct. Try to keep an essay question under, say, five lines at most. The questions, though, need to convey the extent of the focus you want students to address. Again, it is helpful to have a friend or coworker read the question and tell you what he or she understands from it to make sure it is clear.

Marilla D. Svinicki (2002) offers additional practical ideas:

- Prepare the test far enough in advance so you can put the questions away for a day or two and see if they hold up and are clearly written.
- Have a friend proofread the questions.
- Take the test and then multiply the time by four to six, depending upon the level of students.
- Include several types of questions in your tests, and if your test has more than 10 questions, begin with a few of the easier ones to help students orient themselves.

Multiple Choice

If your test will be composed of multiple-choice questions, here are a few ideas to get you started (Svinicki, 2002).

- Write questions instead of statements with blanks, which are harder to devise.
- Don't include irrelevant information.
- Try to avoid negatively phrased questions.
- When creating the choices, write the correct answer first to get your bearings; then develop the distractors.
- If your test has more than 10 questions, begin with a few of the easier ones to help students orient themselves.

Svinicki (2002) suggests you create what she calls a "truth table" with columns and rows labeled true and false as shown in Figure 13.2.

Make sure the language you use is appropriate for your students; read the answers to make sure their syntax blends with that of the question; watch for singular and plural verbs, articles, or adjectives that might give the answer away; and don't make the right answer obviously shorter or longer than the others.

Good tests also have an interior logic that follows a chronology or line of thinking (Svinicki, 2002). We would like students to leave tests feeling they've had a learning experience, that they assembled their knowledge in response to the questions and had an opportunity to express themselves—perhaps even discovering more connections in the process.

FIGURE 13.2
Example of a Truth Table

Stem/Question: What causes the phases of the moon?

	True	*False*
True	The lack of rotation by the moon (correct)	The orbit of the moon around the earth (true, but unrelated)
False	The rotation of the earth (false, but related)	The clouds between the moon and earth (false and unrelated)

Based on a model described in "Test Construction: Some Practical Ideas," in *Teachers and Students: A Sourcebook for UT-Austin Faculty*, by M. D. Svinicki, 2002, Austin: University of Texas at Austin Center for Teaching Effectiveness.

Improvement as a Factor

As you structure your course and determine how much of the final grade will be attached to homework, projects, and exams, you also need to consider whether you will grade on improvement or strict acquisition of knowledge and skill. Sometimes the lines are clear and sometimes they are not.

In order to grade on improvement, a baseline needs to be established. Initial performances and tests generally provide this information. Rubrics can provide guidelines for making a clear assessment of student work at first and later in the term. In some disciplines, a video or audio record may be the right tool to capture early behaviors. Experienced faculty and GSIs may have advice and suggestions for new GSIs regarding the issue of establishing a baseline and of working with the departmental guideline on the percentage of grade for improvement and the percentage assigned to an objective evalua-tion of the quality of work.

Nonnative English Speakers and Others With Writing Problems

Among your international students, you will have some who are nonnative English speakers. Most campuses offer a range of services, including help through trained tutors, drop-in centers, online assistance, or classes for writing, and in some cases, for speaking or reading and listening.[1]

Grading speeches or written texts by nonnative speakers is not a problem once guidelines are established. In some classes, nonstandard grammar means loss of points, regardless of whether the misstep is made by a native or nonnative speaker. Because there are so many successful citizens in the United States who are not native speakers of English, one philosophy may be to note errors but not to mark down for them, because international students are presumably still actively learning English. This method can of course be used with native speakers as well, since they sometimes arrive at college lacking writing skills.

More and more institutions offer writing help of various types and intensities to students through writing centers. Staff at these centers will offer suggestions to you on working with students who have these problems and provide some grading plans.

Weighting Grades

Weighting grades—assigning percentages from the total number of points to homework or quizzes, lab work, classroom participation, projects, and examinations—is another necessity of the system. Which aspects deserve the larger allotment of points?

In addition to dividing the pot, other considerations include an infrequently used variation on weighting grades: give fewer points to early assignments than to later assignments in the same category. The discipline, the experiences and knowledge of the entering students, and the goals of the course are factors to consider for this strategy. I taught a nonfiction writing course in which students wrote five papers worth 20 points each during the semester, except for the first paper. I assigned the first paper a maximum of 10 points and used the other 10 for classroom participation.

My reason for this weighting was that writing is a complex process to teach and to learn, and since students had no idea how I would respond to

---

[1] Trained peer tutors at Agnes Scott College in Decatur, Georgia, meet with students who want help, and a variety of classes are offered at Virginia International University in Fairfax, Virginia, that focus on writing, speaking, reading, and listening.

their work, it seemed fairer to me to reduce the points on the initial assignment.

A sociology professor I knew was so disappointed with the first set of papers he collected from students in a graduate seminar that he discounted the assignment completely—gave them no grade at all. Those students, I suspect, paid strong attention to his writing instructions for their later papers. Any plan of grading that works toward student learning, that is, student-centered teaching, rather than discouraging student effort, is a plan that deserves consideration.

Gatekeeping Knowledge

Gatekeeping knowledge, which is well described in Barbara Walvoord and Virginia Anderson Johnson's book (1998), is a valuable grading concept to keep in mind. If you consider the content of your course and see specific equations, personalities, theories, events, or other material that is absolutely crucial for students to master in order to truly pass the class, then it is perfectly sensible to create a core of information that qualifies as gatekeeping knowledge. Students should be informed of these "red letter" portions of the course and be told that they *must* know these things in order to pass the class. Using this system, an A on three activities and an F on crucial material would not add up to a B minus.

The usefulness of this strategy was illustrated when a GSI for American Sign Language called me one day to express concern about a student who was enrolled in her second-year course. The student, she learned, had done very well on all her written assignments in her first-year course, but "she couldn't sign." The previous teacher had added the student's scores, and the grades on the written work were sufficient for her to pass the class—an especially ironic event for a foreign language.

To employ this grading method, instructors need to give clear explanations to the students about weighting and about gatekeeping content. Students appreciate being told what is of great importance and how important it will be for future learning, so many may welcome your use of the method. When I think of students facing a course with a new stable of knowledge to learn, I think of the experience of moving to a new city, which I've done several times. Initially I see the streets and buildings as relatively equal, but eventually, with tips offered by friends, I learn the important arterials and the landmarks to use in negotiating traffic or locating a particular place or address.

Extra Credit

Whether or not to use extra credit can stir up a lively conversation among instructors. The central debatable point is whether a course is a whole entity and the assignments cover the material fully, or if there are always more roads of inquiry to follow, and if ambitious students should be rewarded for taking on extra work. However, it is not usually the ambitious students who ask about extra credit. Most inquiries come from students who may have neglected regular assignments or who, with the end of the term approaching, see that they are in danger of flunking.

Adding an extra-credit question to a test may be something you'd like to do, because it stretches the students' comprehension of material or asks about an esoteric or intriguing issue tangential to the core of the course, but creating and grading extra assignments or papers is extra work. Give this some thought before classes begin. Your peers probably have some ideas on the subject—possibly some passionately held beliefs.

Grading Attendance

The department may have a strict policy for your students to follow regarding attendance. This policy may include definitions of excused absences: sick with a signed medical form, religious observances, and so forth. If you have some latitude, adopt a structure that lets students have more control. Such a plan will save you time in the long run. An easy version of such a structure is to give students one (or perhaps two, depending upon the total number of meetings) unexcused absences per term. Advise students to save the free zeros for when they are truly needed. Give samples of unexcused absences—a stalled car, a sick roommate, a phone call, a cold—that might be a good cause for missing class. These things are apt to occur. Urge students not to skip class on a whim, so that the "free" absence is available if they need it.

The mechanics of taking attendance has a number of variations. After the first few classes, when the best method is to call names, do a head count. If the number is correct, everyone is there. You also might pass a sheet around for signatures. (Use a sheet with the alphabet printed down the left side so that names will be nearly in order.) Some instructors make a seating chart and assign students to a desk. Humans being who they are, the students themselves may very well adopt a location and stay in it throughout the term. Once you have faces matched with names, you'll be able to mark the roll sheet quickly as students enter or during an activity that occupies them.

Engaged Participation

Whether you are an instructor for Business Leadership, Introduction to Psychology, or Physics for Poets, you should (*should* is a word to avoid, but in the world of teaching as it exists now, it is the correct one) expect your students to participate. And they should expect to do so, too. Participation generally refers to talking, but depending upon your course, it may refer to group work, board problems, courseware entries, or other learning activities.

Some controversy surrounds the issue of whether to grade participation because of the fear that students will say anything to get points or that they will freeze and say nothing because they worry they'll say something stupid. The students for whom mandatory participation is a challenge are those who are shy to a nearly painful degree. Participation doesn't have to mean speaking out in the full class. Contributing to a small-group conversation is easier for some students, and offering rich comments on a Web site bulletin board may be another method of participating.

GSIs will be advised by their professors about whether to grade participation. If you can allot points for "engaged participation," give your students examples of what it means to be engaged and involved in class discussions, small-group activities, and so on. (Refer to the results of what makes a good discussion if your students participated in the activity about creating guidelines described in chapter 7.) Not every student will speak or perform in every class, but over time they all should do so, and they should do it on a regular basis. This clarification will serve everyone well if questions or disputes arise.

Keeping Track of Participation

Once the "whether" hurdle is passed, you have to tackle the "how" hurdle. By far, the simplest method of keeping track of who spoke or otherwise engaged in class activities is to attend to the task immediately after the session.

It is fairly easy to scan your list of students while the hour is fresh and recall, for instance, who spoke and whether their contributions enriched the hour or how well they fulfilled tasks and roles as part of active learning strategies you may have employed. Keep the marking simple. Use a plus to note excellent contributions, a check for small contributions, and leave the spaces of noncontributors blank. If you use a spreadsheet program, enter 3 for outstanding engagement, a 1 for adequate engagement, and a 0 for no engagement so that totals will accumulate and your end-of-term work is reduced. You'll have to determine a final number that fits your class size, number of meetings, and opportunities for engagement. If a class met 20 times and a student offered valuable contributions during 10 of those meetings, that 30 may be a benchmark.

Assessment of Public Speaking

Because most students are not skilled public speakers, be agonizingly clear about your criteria for a good presentation—and you may want to offer the criteria for middling and poor work, too. A rubric may be helpful. Emphasize the importance of gaining competence in making presentations; there are few careers that don't call for some sort of presentation, even if only short reports in meetings.

I suspect that grades are softer in presentations than they are in written work. Our human sympathy kicks in for nervous tics, floundering, and other human foibles. Or we make eye contact with the student and perhaps smile at each other. And then we have a hard time giving them a deserved D.

Avoid this difficulty by offering specific standards. Five minutes should not be 12 minutes or vice versa. You may want to have another student hold up one-minute and one-half-minute cards for the speakers. If students know they will have the warning, they may practice a few more times in order to cover the material they want to include. This arrangement allows you to mark off points for overage, for no conclusion, or for brevity.

It is also crucial that everyone in the room hear the presenter. You should sit in the back of the room. Perhaps you will want to offer one warning about not hearing well by raising your hand. If the student responds for the rest of the talk, he or she should be justly rewarded; receiving a second cue might cause more stress than it is worth.

These directives look harsh on the page, but consider your expectations for written assignments—pages, introduction, supporting evidence, conclusion, bibliography, and so on. Having words or charts or equations on the page makes this task easier in the world of writing. Translating it to talk is a challenge. For instance, we want students to make eye contact with their audience, but do we have a sense of what constitutes an A level of contact, or B level, and so on. At the time of this writing, no classroom device has been promoted as a way to measure eye contact.

Nevertheless, you have to be somewhat intuitive as you assess speeches—even more so than with papers—and every precise point you can give students to let them know the goals they should strive for will benefit them.

The Web has a multitude of forms that assess public speaking, and your department, if it encourages or requires speeches, may have given you a check sheet. It may also be helpful to use the other students. Hand out file cards and ask them to write the speaker's name in the corner and then give them a minute or two after each speech to write out one thing they found excellent about the speech and one way they thought the speaker could improve. Both the student and the instructor should read the cards.

Grading Group Presentations

The details of preparing students for, as well as grading, group presentations are described in chapter 11.

Efficient Grading

It is no small task to grade a stack of 20, 40, or more papers—whether they exist in the courseware system or as a sheaf on your desk. Any tendency GSIs or faculty may have to procrastinate may be quashed by the students' and the administration's expectation that assignments will be returned within a reasonable time. To ease grading time, here are some ideas gleaned from conversations and devised out of necessity over the years. Your peers will have more suggestions.

Blocking Time and Space

An alternative to resolving to grade, say, five papers at a time and then taking a break is to designate blocks of an hour or two for the concentration that grading demands. If you are new to this task, expect that it may feel clumsy initially, and that like most things, you will become more skilled as the term progresses and during your years of teaching.

Depending upon the complications of the assignment, you may want to experiment with skimming through all the papers to assess one aspect, then return later to read for another attribute. This method obviously allows you to gain a good perspective on the level of work your students have done. The key aid for this method is record keeping: develop a grid, a check-off page, another type of form, a verbal recording, or another tool to keep good records on your reactions. If you receive papers via the Web in programs that contain an editing tool, that option may work for you.

Going to a place you designate as a grading location may be helpful, too, such as a campus library you don't use for your research—some place that doesn't have a lot of distractions. For others, the constant clatter of a coffee shop might supply a useful white noise. Location, of course, may depend completely on the medium used for the assignments. You may have no choice but to be at a specific departmental computer or in a lab.

Staggered Due Dates

If you have control over when larger assignments are due, ask students to select one of two dates to turn in their work, so half the work comes in at one time. This smaller pile seems more manageable, and knowing that more will follow in a few days can be a good inspiration to attend to the first stack.

Speed Grading

If you are grading written work, a number of strategies can cut your grading time.

One great tool is a colored marker. If you tend to write a lot of helpful notes in the margin with a pen or pencil, change your method for one set of papers. You'll be able to give students a fast turnaround, which they value highly, and to spend less time on the task. This method is particularly useful for brief assignments or in-class work. Begin by reading quickly through a few papers to assess the types of good or weak answers that students have supplied. Decide on the category of response you want to highlight with your marker and go at it. Without a pen or pencil, you are restricted in the amount of time you spend with a paper because it's virtually impossible to write messages in the margins with fat-tipped markers, especially if they're pale green. You may even be tempted to use two colors to highlight two aspects of student work. When you explain the color code in class, you can offer some general comments about their work and invite follow-up questions then or in later e-mails.

Another strategy is to skim the whole piece but focus on one thing to comment on; faster yet, use a plus, check, or minus sign.

Assessing Grammar

A point alluded to in chapter 10 is that you do not want to wend your way down the long path of the copyeditor or proofreader. The temptation is great, because correcting someone's writing errors is an easy thing to do; those of us who can spell and who can distinguish a compound sentence from a dependent clause feel inclined to show those who don't the errors of their ways. A seminal work in composition research states that students learn grammatical rules more effectively in their own writing rather than as isolated lessons (Braddock, Lloyd-Jones, & Schoer, 1963). Thus, it makes sense to give students help with their grammar problems within their own writing. However, copyediting is enormously time consuming and not necessarily the best strategy. Haswell (as cited in Bean, 2001) reported that students were able to locate and correct about 60% of the errors in their writing when they were guided to where the problems were. Therefore, do the following:

- Put a tick mark at the end of the line where there is an error in that line—misspelling, comma splice, verb disagreement, and so on. Put two or three, if necessary. Let students look for the errors, and even invite them to have a partner look, too, if appropriate for the assignment.
- If the writing is laden with problems, mark only one paragraph or a few sentences, to give the student a sense of the level of errors they need to try to locate on their own. Or, if the writer has lots of problems, mark only one type, and ask the student to see if he or she can locate others of that sort.

My belief is that students with many writing problems have probably been getting papers back with red slashes on them for years, and the student has not learned from previous markups. A new strategy is called for, and giving them more control or power in editing or being analytical may work for some students.

Most colleges and universities have writing centers where students can get one-on-one help. Students should take advantage of the services and not put off the work for a later period in their lives. It is a pity when a résumé is dismissed because a job application letter contains glaring grammatical errors (and even one might do it) that send the whole application into the "no" pile.

Brief and Frequent Assignments

When students turn work in often, the grading needs to be done quickly to keep assignments from piling up and to let students know how they are progressing. It is not uncommon for math instructors to assign, say, five problems and correct only one or two.

Frequent assignments, whether they are problems to be solved or short written pieces that encourage preparedness for class, do not generally need detailed grading. If these assignments are part of an online courseware program, the assigned marks should move into student records with ease.

Surprise Postponement

One novel approach to grading is to surprise students by postponing the due date of their papers. On the day papers are to be handed in, make sure that everyone has brought the assignment. Then announce that they should take them home for a final review.

If students want to make any changes, you might tell them they can use a pen to correct the copy they've printed or tell them to print another version if they like. This technique is especially useful if your students have made a lot of sloppy errors in the past. A delay gives them an opportunity to proof-read again and improve their grade; if they turn in better papers, it will save you time, too.

Some students may feel that they've done the best work they can do and want to pass it in immediately; they may even resent other students' getting an extension. If you want to avoid any grumbles, you could allow the postponement for a two-point penalty (out of a hundred points), for instance, which a lot of them might still take, since they may gain much more than they'll lose.

Another unexpected event would be to collect papers and then hand them out to others in class for a quick peer review before inviting students to take them home for modifications. I suggest that you use this strategy only once in a term, but you may think of other ways to surprise your students a time or two on other matters.

Marginalia or Endnotes

Many GSIs and faculty mark up papers within the text as well as writing notes at the end. You might try one or the other, especially on shorter essays. Most instructors give papers that are 10 to 15 pages in length marginalia and a note at the end. The students' hard work merits the attention. This method of grading a paper allows you to attend to small and major issues, but expect to spend 20 to 40 minutes or more to grade a complex assignment.

The following contains some suggestions to shorten the time it takes you to respond to papers.

Making Use of Technology

Consider writing your comments on a computer, either in an e-mail or to print out, and give a copy to the student with his or her paper. If you want to make marginal comments, write numbers in the margin and circle them next to the text you are questioning, then on a separate piece of paper, type your comments in a list next to the corresponding numbers. You can obviously write more in a shorter time this way. Some instructors write an assessment paragraph about the essay without any marginalia, staple it to the paper, and return it.

If your computer has a microphone, you may want to use software that allows you to record comments about a student's paper while you're reading it. Add circled letters in the margin for reference points, if appropriate. With practice this method of response will reduce your grading time and/or let you give students more complete feedback about their work. Students, of course, need the capability of listening to your comments. You could also burn comments on a CD or record into an audiocassette. Some coursewares, such as Blackboard, have this capability as well. If this method works well for you, ask students to provide a read-write disk to be used throughout the course.

Susan Sipple (2006) from the University of Cincinnati Raymond Walters College has been recording comments for students for 16 years and reports that she can provide more extensive and clearer feedback.[2] She also

---

[2] She began with audiotapes and now records audio CDs for students or e-mails them MP3 files. She recommends Sound Forge as an editing tool.

believes that creating a conversation about the paper helps students understand her comments more thoroughly and positively. In a small study, students revised more completely with audio comments than they did with written notes.

Templates

If you prefer or need to grade by writing comments, you may find that using a template to indicate recurring problems saves you time. After a few assignments you may find yourself repeating advice, such as "Evidence presented is not well connected to main argument. See _____" or "Double-check formulas. See _____" Fill in the blanks with the letters or numbers that match reference points in the margins of the student's work. GSIs may be able to construct such a list with other GSIs who are teaching sections for the same professor.

These sheets can seem impersonal to students, so let them know that you use the checklist for common problems so that you'll have more time to add particularized comments to their assignments. Show them the list ahead of time to illustrate problems that occur frequently. Like a rubric, the list may help students avoid the problems in the first place.

Timers

A timer—kitchen, computer, sports—can be a great boost in tending to papers. If you are grading papers that you believe ought to occupy about fifteen minutes each, set the timer appropriately. When it rings, you may not be completely finished, but you will have a reminder that you've reached a period that you had judged as sufficient. This strategy is especially helpful when you are grading a poor paper, and you find yourself marking up more and more things to justify a D or F. Stop. Pretty soon you'll be spending more time on the paper than the student did.

Grade Complaints

The first line of advice for handling grade complaints is that if a student wants to dispute a grade, make an appointment to discuss it so you are not caught off guard having a grade conversation in the hall. In my early days of teaching, I passed back the students' first papers, which had a 20-point possibility. As I was packing up my materials and talking with other students, one young woman shoved her paper in front of my face (it had a 16) and asked why she hadn't received all 20 points. I was a bit rattled, and I realized that I needed a system to handle questions.

You GSIs may want to develop a system that includes a time gap so that you will be able to consult with your teaching supervisor if necessary. You may also want to have the complaint and the paper left with you overnight so that you can review it without the impatient sighs from a testy student who's sitting across the desk from you. Your department may have a policy to follow, too.

I know a faculty member who teaches large classes who developed a complaint system that requires students to hand write an explanation of the complaint, which they cannot hand in until two days after receiving the grade. She reviews the complaint and then makes an appointment with the student. The time factor and the need to write out the complaint make the discussion less emotional and more productive; she also suspects that the protocol discourages some students who might be inclined to register a complaint in the heat of the moment.

Student Evaluations of You

Reviewing your student evaluations can be a trying experience. You may have felt that the students were very happy with the class, but the evaluations may reveal some unexpected and previously unexpressed dissatisfaction. Because the course has ended, you cannot speak to class members again or try to fix whatever troubled them. During another semester, you may want to give a midterm assessment or other types of classroom assessments (see chapter 5), so you can modify your teaching methods during the term.

It is a success to see 90% to 95% satisfaction among students. If you have only one or two outliers, be content with your effort, though that can be easier said than done. If complaints centered on one or two teaching methods, the best thing to do is to resolve to experiment with other teaching strategies. If you have a number of troubling or unexpected responses, discuss them with your teaching supervisor or make an appointment with someone in the faculty development office.

If students raised objections to something you found effective and that you thought was beneficial for the class, you may want to modify the way you use it or reconsider how you introduce the strategy. I knew a GSI who insisted her students write three pages daily as part of their writing course. Many students found it rewarding, but a few of them balked. At the beginning of the new term, she brought in a student from a previous class to talk about the positive effects the student had from this daily writing assignment. The GSI said the student testimonial was so helpful that she made it a regular part of her writing classes from that point forward.

Grading is one of the most complex and important parts of instruction. Done well, it should offer students guidance, not punishment, and it should inform your teaching, too. As with assignments, creative options abound.

References

Bean, J. C. (2001). *Engaging ideas: A professor's guide to integrating writing, critical thinking, and active learning in the classroom.* San Francisco: Jossey-Bass.

Braddock, R., Lloyd-Jones, R., & Schoer, L. (1963). *Research in written composition.* Urbana, IL: National Council of Teachers of English.

Jenkins, A., & Unwin, D. (1996). *How to write learning outcomes.* National Center for Geographic Information and Analysis. Retrieved October 10, 2006, from http://www.ncgia.ucsb.edu /education / curricula / giscc / units / format / outcomes .html

Sipple, S. (2006, August 16). Digitized audio commentary in first year writing classes. *Academic Commons.* Retrieved January 28, 2007, from http://www .academiccommons.org/crfi/vignette/digitized-audio-commentary

Svinicki, M. D. (2002). Test construction: Some practical ideas. *Teachers and students: A sourcebook for UT-Austin faculty.* University of Texas at Austin Center for Teaching Effectiveness. Retrieved December 3, 2007, from http://www.utexas .edu/academic/cte/sourcebook/tests.pdf

Walvoord B., & Johnson Anderson, V. (1998). *Effective grading: A tool for learning and assessment.* San Francisco: Jossey-Bass.

14

MAKING THE MOST OF YOUR TEACHING TIME AND PLANNING FOR YOUR FUTURE

Both GSIs and new faculty look ahead to the next phase: employment or tenure. For GSIs, teaching may play a major part in their future. For faculty in large institutions, research and publications will influence tenure more than teaching, but for those in smaller liberal arts colleges, teaching plays a larger role in evaluation. Despite the range of variation, developing a **Teaching Portfolio** in which you organize your records will serve you well regardless of what comes next. Other activities that support efforts to obtain employment or tenure are **Papers, Poster Sessions, Awards, and More**. Aimed particularly at GSIs who do not expect to teach, understanding how **Translating Teaching Experiences Into a Career Other Than Teaching** will help you think about ways this experience can benefit your plans, including details such as whether to submit a **Résumé or Curriculum Vitae** to a prospective employer.

Teaching Portfolios

A teaching portfolio is designed to give shape to the accumulated experiences of your teaching. The elements of a portfolio include a philosophy of teaching and copies of syllabi, assignments, letters from faculty supervisors (GSIs) or department heads (faculty), descriptions of awards, student evaluations, and so on. While you might think that it makes sense to develop a portfolio after a few years of teaching (many people do just that), you will be well served to begin creating your portfolio during your first semester of teaching.

Peter Seldin's (2004) book on teaching portfolios details the contents of a portfolio and offers dozens of examples of various elements. The book developed out of his work with faculty members seeking tenure or promotion, so the portfolios reflect years of courses, committee work, advising, and other activities of faculty, but beyond the scope of GSIs' experiences. Nevertheless the book offers valuable insights and suggestions for instructors, regardless of where they are in their careers.

A teaching philosophy, which is a key part of a portfolio and many job applications, is not an easy document to write. Teaching is complex, and one's ideas and teaching practices shift. Also, unlike, say, a philosophy about food or watching television, most people don't articulate their philosophy of teaching very often.

An approach to drafting a philosophy of teaching might begin with an exercise like the one on written assignments, p. 135 in chapter 10, composing a thinking paper. Keep the document you draft in a readily available place on your computer so that when an important new thought or phrase or an idea about revision occurs to you, you can easily attend to it.

A philosophy statement should be personal, free of most jargon, and reflect you and your teaching experiences. The text should be roughly one page long. In order to create a statement that truly reflects you and the way you teach, Seldin advises against reading a philosophy from someone in your discipline until your own essay seems completed. "Complete" is relative here, since you will very likely alter it as you have more teaching experiences and acquire a richer language to express thoughts about instruction.

When I've advised people on ways to discover their personal beliefs about teaching, I ask them to write about

- a teacher (from any time in their past) whom they admired
- the moment or period in their lives when they experienced the "wow" realization about what they wanted to study
- the events leading up to that moment
- an imagined discussion at a cocktail party where a friend of the family approaches them and denigrates their field

These writing exercises can draw out feelings and attitudes about one's field, admired characteristics of a teacher and methods of teaching that the instructor aspires to or emulates, and language to defend the importance of one's discipline within the world of education and within the world. The results of these writing exercises composes the raw material to develop a philosophy that describes the what and the why.

As you work to make your essay personal, steer clear of the clichés in education, such as "empowerment" and even "active learning" and "critical thinking." Everyone believes that critical thinking is important for students to master, but the term has been overused. Rather than saying you promote critical thinking or employ active learning techniques, discuss an assignment or a method of teaching you use to illustrate how you guide students to expand their growth in thinking. Then if you mention critical thinking or active learning, the terms are connected to authentic events and pedagogical methods that you practice.

GSIs should know that it has become more and more common for institutions to request teaching philosophies with job applications. An entire portfolio is requested less frequently, but if you prepare one, you will not only have a packet ready if it is requested, you will also find that the process of preparing it provides excellent preparation for interview questions relating to teaching. Many of the GSIs I worked with told me that gathering and evaluating material and then writing about it was a big asset for interviews. Several of them said that they felt that creating the portfolio contributed strongly to their obtaining a teaching job.

New faculty will learn about the tenure process early in their career, perhaps even before they take a new position. Your institution will probably require some version of a portfolio to review your teaching. Another point to consider is that you may or may not stay at the institution where you begin your career. A portfolio will be a helpful tool for your search for a new position.

Another element that I suggest job seekers include in their portfolio is a well-annotated list of courses they would like to teach and/or would feel confident teaching. In addition to relying on your academic strengths, browse through the targeted college catalog to find courses that you feel you could manage or prepare for in a reasonable length of time.

GSIs must take care in regard to the way they promote themselves for a position. Despite the strong desire to obtain a job, be honest about expressing yourself in every aspect of your job application and interview. I counseled a GSI who was afraid of revealing his beliefs regarding aspects of the discipline during the interview because he thought he would not get the position. I told him about a Marxist economist I knew who had interviewed at a small college where the economics department was composed of three professors, and two of them were searching for a third. The man lived his discipline and, since he was ambivalent about the job, presented himself as he was—a polar opposite to the two Keynesian economists in the department. They were delighted to be able to bring in a voice that so broadened their small department, and the trio thrived for several years. That anecdote, along with my urging the GSI to realize that he would be miserable working for an institution that wanted another type of person, persuaded him to present himself as he was. The job search had a happy ending; he found a position where he felt both welcome and accepted.

Along with working on a draft of a teaching philosophy, create a physical folder where you can accumulate papers—syllabi, assignments, letters, and so on. During the term, makes notes about successful classroom activities, assignments that resulted in excellent work from students, or a flop that you salvaged. When the term ends, open the appropriate file(s) on your computer and describe a few of these classroom moments on your syllabus or on an assignment page. Your syllabus may grow by a page from your additions, but those who review your materials will feel suddenly engaged with you in a discussion about classroom experiences. When you are ready to submit teaching materials for a position or tenure review, highlight your commentaries in yellow and then staple a small note to the front page directing readers to note the highlighted sections for commentary specific to a topic, activity, or assignment.

Sometimes GSIs ask whether they should add notes or e-mails from students—praise that arrives unexpectedly and includes things such as, "Your class was one of the best I've ever taken." Employers know that applicants submit rosy material, and they can guess that you would omit a note with the opposite sentiment, but I believe it cannot hurt to include a few such notes when they are spontaneous and unsolicited. Faculty should omit such things from tenure review packets unless they are explicitly invited.

Student evaluations are another matter. In Seldin's (2004) examples, some professors created a table with summaries of questions, course title and year, and numerical results. This sort of efficient summary will probably be required by tenure committees and they will be appreciated by hiring committees. (When sending such information for review to another institution, be sure to note the scale of your numbers, as some schools use a 5.0 scale and others use a 6.0.) Occasionally hiring committees ask for copies of the official data printouts of student evaluations rather than a grid of the totals, and once I was told about a school that wanted every sheet marked by a student plus copies of their responses to open-ended questions, which are part of some end-of-term evaluations and include questions such as, "Would you recommend this instructor to other students? Why or why not?" In this instance, the GSI had taught for five years and had inches of evaluations. Sometimes your department will bear the cost of photocopying, and sometimes GSIs have to pay for it. Some departments keep all instructors' evaluations and others turn the forms over to the teachers. I've met more than one GSI who hadn't realized the importance of saving the forms and had tossed them. Summaries can be recovered from the data center, but it's obviously easier to save everything until you have the position you want.

Other commonly included documents in the portfolio are letters from supervising faculty (for GSIs) and department chairs who may sit in on your classes now and then. If your supervisor praises your teaching, ask for a letter for your file. Faculty members and chairs are accustomed to writing letters of recommendation or commendation.

You may also have occasion to invite a staff member from your faculty development office to come to your class to perform a classroom assessment as described in chapter 5. Such a visit generally leads to a visit with the staff member and some documentation, which, if positive, should definitely be included in a portfolio.

The documents you will want to collect for your portfolio, then, are a teaching philosophy, descriptions of courses and teaching methods, and information on evaluations. Letters, awards, descriptions of participation in regional or national meetings within your discipline also deserve to be included. After the few pages of description, add an appendix with the appropriate raw material.

Beyond classroom and discipline activities, GSIs should watch for opportunities that would occupy a small amount of time but add another line on the résumé. An example might be appearing on a panel discussion for alumni or new parents or prospective students. Participating in events of this type shows a willingness to extend yourself beyond your appointment. Faculty often have a certain amount of required work of this kind, but if you're new to the campus, it will still be beneficial to stay apprised of campus and community activities where opportunities may present themselves. Of course, GSIs who work with a professor on his or her research project should seek to develop a conference presentation. Poster sessions and presentations are an important activity in academia, and the sooner you can participate in such events, the better.

Papers and Poster Sessions, Awards, and More

Shortly after entering graduate school, if not before, GSIs will become familiar with the professional societies and associations of their discipline. New faculty will arrive with connections in place. Many of these groups have List-servs, which will keep you informed about regional and national meetings, publications, and activities of your professional peers. Their Web sites also advertise conferences and other events.

New GSIs should ask faculty supervisors or other professors for advice on ways to contribute or submit proposals or otherwise participate in the discipline's community. Experienced GSIs may have suggestions, too, but if they try to discourage you (as can happen with those who have not had great success in their own efforts), seek information elsewhere. GSIs need to remember that the department admitted you under the assumption that you would be a fine student and a graduate it would be proud of. Becoming a scholar takes time, and all progress you can make during your graduate career will serve you after you have your degree. Your institution wants you to be successful while you are a student, and it wants you to obtain a desirable position when you complete your work.

New faculty, too, need to ask a number of peers about opportunities. In some institutions, you will be paired with a senior faculty member in some type of mentoring relationship. Many colleges have departments or personnel who help faculty locate appropriate grants and assist with writing proposals. Your new employers want you to be an excellent teacher and a fine scholar, and they will be especially pleased if you produce work that brings good attention to you and the institution or if you bring grant money to support your research, because it also supports the institution. To this end, many resources are available for faculty. Take advantage of them.

Papers and Poster Sessions

Obviously, publications or their equivalents are the key method of gaining tenure at research universities. New faculty are all too aware of the work they must accomplish in the first five or six years at a big institution if they want to receive tenure. GSIs may have fewer opportunities to research and publish (given their full responsibilities), but if you can work with a professor in his or her research, try to make time for it. It is obviously beneficial to have your name on a publication before you graduate.

Poster sessions can provide another way to publicize research findings (based perhaps on work in a seminar or a portion of a project with a professor) and gain a listing at a conference. Notifications of conferences are generally posted on your department's bulletin board, and of course the discipline's Web site offers information that may include advice on how best to create posters, specific areas of interest within the discipline, and relevant conferences.

Graduate colleges, as the umbrella organization for many services as well as requirements for graduate students, offer assistance of many kinds. Four services they may offer are

- courses or seminars to help in writing dissertations
- funds for travel costs or conference registration fees
- lists of campus opportunities for teaching and research positions
- information on internships, fellowships, and scholarships

Grants for international opportunities may be another administrative arm of your institution. If the Graduate College in your school doesn't manage the items above, it should be able to direct you to the right office.

Awards

Awards are another valuable asset on a job application or in a tenure review packet. Apply for recognition of classroom instruction or projects you have done. Sometimes articles receive commendation in a publication or from a larger organization. In some instances this recognition arrives without your expecting it, but in many instances you have to apply in some way, so be alert for opportunities whether they are local, regional, or national, or inside or beyond your discipline. Any form of recognition may be valuable in your career as well as providing the possibility of making connections with others in your field.

Letters

Again, GSIs are urged to remember to ask for letters. If you have completed a course, particularly one where you worked on a large project and you did so brilliantly, ask your professor for a letter. You may want it in your "career services" file or your grant application file. Obtaining it sooner than later is not only helpful to the faculty member who has your work fresh in mind but will help you avoid the dreaded feeling of asking for a letter on short notice to meet a deadline.

Translating Teaching Experience Into a Career Other Than Teaching

This section is for GSIs who have no intention of teaching after graduate school. Business majors rarely see teaching in their future, and likewise for those in engineering, administration, or nonprofit management.

Regardless of your career goals, many aspects of teaching will contribute to wisdom and skills you can use elsewhere. Teaching in college allows you to practice many skills that are valued in the business world or government service, to name two categories. These might include

- project management
- material selection and use
- media preparation and use
- planning and setting long-term goals
- aligning goals with a timeline
- abiding by time constraints to achieve short-term goals
- running meetings
- managing a group of disparate people
- coaching people who are learning
- correcting people who get the answer wrong
- creating assessment tools
- evaluating performance
- presenting material

A few of these points, elaborated on below, offer some ideas about how to match teaching experiences to activities in business.

Developing a course and creating a syllabus can and should certainly be described as project management. This term is often associated with corporations, but in fact projects are part of every position. Each project has some sort of relationship to a calendar, each one has interior goals, and each one requires oversight.

Another commonality from teaching that applies to many positions would be material selection and use. In teaching, books, print resources, Web sites, shareware, media, laboratory materials or the studio tools of art and music, and so on are the standard learning aids. People are another resource—guest speakers, interview subjects, and so on. Finally, you may have become skilled in selecting and making arrangements to use locations; urban planners sit on curbs and observe traffic patterns, archaeologists spend their time at dig sites, curators analyze museum space, and on it goes. Regardless of the limits you may have in your teaching, the experience of locating, selecting, and determining the use of materials provides practice and background for performing these tasks in other positions.

A major activity of teaching is, to put it simply, *managing people*—singly or in groups. Teaching activities require coaching, setting and enforcing deadlines, dealing with complaints as well as trying to avoid them, and performing evaluations. Depending upon the kind of professional positions you may obtain, one major difference could rest in the area of authority. The gap between teacher and student is generally fairly wide—at least in the formal design, but every school has levels of administrators and support staff, too. In the ideal workplace, people often perform their tasks much more like peers or team members, even if one person is the manager. But most offices have a hierarchy, and teaching prepares you for such a structure.

Becoming skilled in running a classroom means that you have learned how to deal with varying types of social dynamics, which is a key ability for people who manage offices or run meetings. Finally, the many ways that GSIs need to meet deadlines translates well into the goals of any type of enterprise.

As you work on your job application materials and you consider how teaching activities translate into the job description before you, think broadly. With luck, your future employer will be impressed with your skill in understanding that the processes of many leadership positions have a great deal in common.

Résumé or Curriculum Vitae

What sort of position will you be looking for? Businesses want a résumé, which is a brief summary of education, jobs, and extracurricular activities, while institutions of higher education expect a curriculum vitae (CV).

The one-page résumé that has been put forth as the ideal in recent years also contains a "career goal" at the top. You will learn from your peers, faculty advisors, the career center, and employers who visit the campus about the advised length and type of résumé most desirable for your field.

If you do not have to abide by the requirement of a single page for the positions you apply for, let your activities dictate the length. Once you've completed four or five years in graduate school, you may have been a GSI for six different courses, a senior GSI for teams of new GSIs, an assistant in several research projects, contributed relevant columns to the campus newspaper, and organized seminars or other campus events. You may have published an article or presented papers in a discipline-specific journal or participated in a blog or created a podcast.

Employers want to know the breadth of your experiences and the amount of initiative you exercised in them. Regarding teaching, you probably know that being a GSI on one campus can signify a far different set of responsibilities than on another campus or in another discipline. Be succinct, but summarize *all* of your responsibilities. Proofread your résumé as if you resided hundreds of miles away at an institution that is as different from yours as you can imagine, or better yet ask a relative or friend who is not associated with your school to read your résumé and raise questions about anything that is puzzling.

A vita, or curriculum vitae, is the standard way to submit your academic activities to an institution of higher learning. The focus of this document should be your education, your scholarly research and accomplishments, and your teaching. Offer all relevant details pertaining to your dissertation and to articles and presentations, conferences attended, and so on. The hiring committee reviewing this document wants to see people who understand the road to tenure and have already set some research guideposts for themselves. The committee wants to hire someone its institution will be proud to have on the faculty, both for the candidate's work in professional societies and for valued scholarship in the field. If this scholarship is a tool for attracting grant money or creating praiseworthy art, so much the better.

Finally, more graduates are placing their CVs or résumés on the Web. Whether this method is a standard for your discipline will become known to you as you talk with peers who are actively applying for positions. The Web easily allows you to add film clips or CAD animations or other demonstrations of your work that a position requires. It is becoming more common for schools to allot space to job-seeking-graduates and to offer guidance in downloading material.

GSIs may feel that it is an impossible task to begin thinking about the future beyond graduate school with all the time currently required by classes, teaching, and whatever activities of life that are squeezed in around the edges. Do what you can to approach small pieces of it. When more time becomes available or deadlines begin to press on you, you'll be grateful for whatever you've been able to draft and accumulate up to that point.

New faculty members have completed many of the steps of this chapter and built their own path to obtaining a position. GSIs should consult with new faculty members about the process of applying and hiring. GSIs who graduate and gain a teaching position at a university will be grateful that they have already created a portfolio. Your new institution may require one as part of the tenure process, and you'll be glad to have a head start on its creation.

Reference

Seldin, P. (2004). *Teaching portfolio: A practical guide to improved performance and promotion/tenure decisions* (3rd ed.). Williston, VT: Anker.